D1499994

LESSONS FROM THE BIG GUYS

What I Learned from Servant Leaders
JACK ECKERD, BILL LEE, HUGH McCOLL,
AND ADOLPH RUPP

BILLY O. WIREMAN

President Emeritus, Queens University of Charlotte

FOREWORD BY DICK GOODE AND BOB WHALEN

NEWSOUTH BOOKS
MONTGOMERY

NewSouth Books
P.O. Box 1588
Montgomery, AL 36102

Library of Congress Cataloging-in-Publication Data

ISBN 1-58838-086-6

Design by Randall Williams
Printed in the United States of America

WINGED HORSES THAT NEVER TIRE

Great risk does not take hold of a spineless man.
And if you must die, why squat in the shadows
And coddle a bland, nameless old age,
Deprived of nobility for nothing.
No! I'll undertake this exploit, and (to a god)
I pray, let me achieve it.
He spoke and his words found their target.
For the god honored him with the gift of
A golden chariot and
winged horses that never tire.

— PINDAR

CONTENTS

FOREWORD

DICK GOODE AND BOB WHALEN

This is the story of an adventure, an odyssey, in leadership. It is the story of how a kid born in 1932 in Quicksand, Kentucky, became, in his day, the youngest college president in America, and how he learned to lead.

But this is not really a story about him but rather about his four extraordinary teachers and what they taught him. The "Big Guys," Wireman calls them. And they are big, in personality, ambition, talent, drive, and accomplishment. Whether these "Big Guys" intended it or not, they got up every day and put into practice a style and philosophy of doing things that many today call "servant leadership."

In this book, Billy Wireman identifies the characteristics of his four mentors and shows how anyone can adopt their practices and build a style of effective leadership.

The story begins in 1957 when a very young Billy Wireman met his first teacher, the master of basketball, Adolph Rupp, who launched Wireman's leadership odyssey.

The odyssey continued for more than forty years, during which Billy Wireman also met and learned from Jack Eckerd, the king of retail; Bill Lee, the world's nuclear engineer; and Hugh McColl, America's premier banker.

A natural leader himself, Wireman realized from the

beginning of his career that leadership and service go hand-in-hand. Fate having placed him in a position to learn from these extraordinary "Big Guys," he resolved to be a student of leadership and to put the lessons into practice. This he has done.

Significantly, Billy Wireman has led virtually every organization in which he has been involved: Captain or co-captain of high school and college athletic teams, president of his college fraternity, editor of an antiaircraft battalion newspaper—*The Tracer*—as an intelligence officer in the Marine Corps. Further, he chaired both the Charlotte Community Relations Committee and The Charlotte World Affairs Council. And, additionally, he was president of both Eckerd College and Queens University of Charlotte. Currently, he chairs an advisory committee for the Charlotte public schools to bring six magnet schools to the system around the theme of "Leadership for Global Economics." For a number of years he gave the wrap-up lecture to General Electric's Top Management Seminar at Ossining, New York. He served two terms on the board of directors for The American Management Associations and lectured frequently in the AMA's "Operation Enterprise," a leadership program for college students.

In 1969, he was named one of the "Outstanding Young Men in America." In 2001, he received "The Lifetime Leadership Award" from Leadership Charlotte, and in 2003, he was honored as "Charlottean of the Year" by the Charlotte Easter Seals Society.

He has lectured and been a consultant for various foundations, the U.S. State Department and The United Board for Christian Higher Education in Asia, on every continent save

Australia and Antarctica. He also leads student study tours from Queens to Asia, Russia, and Europe.

Billy Wireman has given two academic institutions new life: Once financially strapped, Eckerd College is now one of America's premier liberal arts colleges, and a struggling all-female Queens College is now fully coed Queens University of Charlotte, consistently ranked as one of the South's leading universities. His three hundred articles, essays, speeches, and book reviews have appeared in the *St. Petersburg Times, Charlotte Observer, Charlotte Business Journal, Miami Herald, New York Times, Vital Speeches of the Day*, and numerous journals. Additionally, he and his colleagues have authored six books.

Pindar's poem conveys something of this servant leadership adventure—great risk, nobility of purpose, and lessons in leadership, lessons in living, that became for Billy Wireman "winged horses that never tire."

We, together with Tamara Dickson, Billy Wireman's indefatigable assistant for a number of years, have helped Billy Wireman tell this remarkable story, but the words and the story are his. We were inspired by it. We think you will be, too.

To Travel Hopefully

*"Hook your wagon to a star, Billy. Associate with capable
people of integrity who are going somewhere."*

—MARY CECIL BACH
MY MATERNAL GRANDMOTHER, 1941

"To travel hopefully is a better thing than to arrive."

—ROBERT LOUIS STEVENSON
El Dorado

A merica and the world need a new kind of leader. Terrorist
attacks, corporate corruption, church scandals, the challenges of globalization in the new millennium, they all call on
us to rethink what we should expect of our leaders. The
leadership ethos of a not too distant past, that narrow-spirited,
self-absorbed, "how-to-get-what-you-want," "I-want-it-all-and-
I-want-it-now," "me-first" sort of leadership will only lead us
deeper into the pit of self-delusion, despair, and destruction.

We don't so much need new leaders as we need a new ethic
of leadership.

We desperately need Servant Leadership.

Servant leadership is not my idea. A generation ago, Robert

Greenleaf defined the phrase in his classic book, *Servant Leadership: A Journey into the Nature of Legitimate Power & Greatness*. Greenleaf's vision of leadership has spread, quietly and powerfully, through some but not nearly enough of our institutions. Hundreds of people, more eloquent than I, have urged us all to hearken to Greenleaf's call. I add my voice to theirs.

Here's why: Greenleaf's definition of servant leadership is a powerful and beautiful example of precisely the kind of leadership that we critically need right now:

> The servant-leader is servant first. . . . Servant leadership begins with the natural feeling that one wants to serve, to serve first. Then conscious choice brings one to aspire to lead. That person is sharply different from one who is leader first, perhaps because of the need to assuage an unusual power drive or to acquire material possessions. The leader-first and the servant-first are two extreme types. . . . The difference manifests itself in the care taken by the servant—first to make sure that other people's highest priority needs are being served. The best test, and difficult to administer, is this: Do those served grow as persons? Do they, *while being served*, become healthier, wiser, freer, more autonomous, more likely to become servants? *And* what is the effect on the least privileged in society? Will they benefit or at least not be further deprived?

Greenleaf concludes with an undeniable reality: "Everything begins with the initiative of an individual."

In this little book, I sketch four portraits of servant leadership. Four more different or unlikely servant leaders you will never meet. They were rough and tumble wrestlers in the world's arena. Ferocious, fractious, hardheaded, opinionated, impatient, and incandescently ambitious, they could be equally caring and nurturing. They didn't suffer fools lightly. While each would scoff at the very idea that he was some sort of saint, time and again they stepped forth to help people in need.

Thus, this effort is not about leadership theory; it's not a how-to book; it's not a self-improvement model. Rather, it's a profile of four remarkable servant leaders whose careers intersected my own for five decades, each of whom fulfilled admirably Greenleaf's definition of servant leadership. As each of these leaders rose to the top of his profession, he manifested Greenleaf's point that, "everything begins with the initiative of an individual."

The initiatives of my four mentors altered, in one case, the face of basketball in America; in another case, the retail drug business; in a third case, the outlook for nuclear energy; and, in a fourth case, American banking. More importantly, through their deep sense of civic responsibility, Adolph Rupp, Jack Eckerd, Bill Lee, and Hugh McColl helped to ensure that their communities were "healthier, wiser, and freer." The incalculably rich endowments they bequeathed to America were possible because each had the traits of Pindar's "winged horses that never tire."

LEADERSHIP IS A BAFFLING CONCEPT, perhaps the most studied and least understood idea in the human enterprise.

Many of us have known that terrible, and wonderful, moment: all eyes in the group turn toward you, and they seem to be all the eyes in the world, and say, "Well, you're the leader; you're responsible now—what do we do next?"

You're the leader—in kindergarten, at a church camp, in your synagogue, at the PTA, the civic club, of your bowling team. You're the one in charge—you've got to make the arrangements, make the decisions—you're responsible. You've got to get things organized, get jobs coordinated, inspire the troops. You're the scoutmaster, the second lieutenant, the office manager, the team captain, the pastor, the teacher, the vice president, and often the father and the mother, too. And, yes, even the president. It's up to you. If things work, you're the hero. If they fail, you're the goat.

Some crave that moment. Others live in terror of it. Most of us experience some mixture of the two. But humans live in communities, and communities inevitably have leaders. Leadership is integral to human life. Little wonder then that we humans are fascinated by leadership. Library shelves groan under books about it. Written human history began as tales about great or notorious leaders: Who can forget the Bible story of young David slaying Goliath? Or Moses leading his people out of Egypt? Or Alexander the Great, who conquered Persia, only to be murdered at age thirty-three by his own warriors?

Our leaders become objects of our admiration or scorn, models of what to do, warnings against what not to do. Great leaders can inspire us by great words or great deeds—consider Thomas Jefferson's "All men are created equal"; Abraham Lincoln's famous "With malice toward none, with charity toward all"; Franklin Roosevelt's "The only thing we have to fear is fear itself"; Martin Luther King, Jr.'s "I Have A Dream";

and Mother Teresa's heroic efforts in the slums of Calcutta. Who hasn't marveled at Joan of Arc's heroic stand, only to be burned at the stake? Awful leaders can wreak horrifying damage: Hitler and the Holocaust, the tens of millions of Russian deaths caused by Lenin and Stalin, and Pol Pot's carnage in Cambodia. Think of Iraq's Saddam Hussein who brought untold hardship and countless deaths to his people. And consider Osama bin Laden, so riddled with religious hate that he sends young followers on suicide missions to kill innocent people.

Who we are, how we live, what we desire, and what we achieve, are all profoundly shaped by our leaders, and by our leadership.

To an extraordinary degree, each of my mentors embodied Greenleaf's concept of Servant Leadership—to **serve first**, and then lead: to make people who **served** with them "healthier, freer, wiser."

To be sure, there is no shortage of theories of leadership, and all share valuable insights. Undoubtedly, for instance, certain personality traits, certain temperaments—decisiveness, energy, vision, command presence, intuition—make some persons more effective leaders than others. This is known as the "trait" concept of leadership. Significantly, Hitler and Lenin had all of these qualities. Clearly, these were not enough.

It's also important to distinguish between "managers," who can carry out orders efficiently, and "leaders" who can envision the orders needed to accomplish the mission, and inspire others to carry them out—to get things done through, and with, others. Some leaders are "authoritarian" leaders, whose power rests on some combination of tradition and coercion; some are "legitimate" leaders who are followed because they are perceived as acting efficiently and effectively in everyone's welfare; some leaders are indeed "charismatic" leaders, who seem to possess some kind of supernatural "magic." Castro is charismatic, and Mussolini's efficiency had the trains running on time. Obviously, a leadership style can be grossly misguided and impoverished.

Leadership has also been defined simply as the capacity to rally others to a cause and then mobilize the human and fiscal resources to achieve the goal. Millions of Germans rallied to Hitler's orations. But, again, where is the moral base?

Then there is the "transformational" versus the "transactional" ideas of leadership. Transformational leaders gather up what they have inherited and transform it into a new vision, a new paradigm. Transactional leaders merely move around what they have with little thought for a plan to improve the situation.

Some people become leaders because of the crises they endure, the adventures they undertake, become representative of others' crises and adventures. Such leaders then become "role models" for the rest of us. The heroic response of former Mayor Rudy Giuliani following the horrific September 11 disaster comes to mind. The Mayor rose to the occasion and made all of us proud to be American. Yes, the times often really do "make the man or woman." Context is extremely important. At certain historical moments people arise to leadership because they have the temperament, the vision, the passion, needed at that moment—Franklin Roosevelt's "New Deal," Ronald Reagan's "Morning in America," and John Kennedy's "New Frontier" come to mind. President George Bush's "Compassionate Conservatism" has rallied millions of Americans. One doesn't have to agree with every element of these ideas to acknowledge that they struck at the deeper chords of America's character and strength. They "held out hope and stirred people's souls to noble ends," in the words of one political analyst.

Historian Will Durant, in his book *The Lessons of History*, offers this insightful observation on leadership: "What determines whether a challenge will or will not be met, the answer is that this depends upon the presence or absence of initiative and of creative individuals with clarity of mind and energy of will capable of effective responses to new situations." This type of leadership—"clarity of mind and energy of will"—let's agree, makes all the difference in the world for good or evil. Great leaders—like Nelson Mandela, who said, on his release from prison after twenty-seven years, "I don't have time for revenge; I need everyone's help in building this great country"—transform their worlds in creative, fruitful, love-filled ways. Perverse leaders—Milosovic and Stalin—can work unimaginable destruction. Leadership can be trivialized into mere celebrity; people gain influence not because of their character or their accomplishments but because they are notorious, because the mass media has flashed its vast light on them and transformed them, for the moment, into pseudo-leaders.

Today more than ever we need neither communist-style "personality cults" nor fascist "Fuhrers" nor "Caudillos" nor "Duces." What we need are models of democratic leadership, the leadership of, for example, Myanmar's heroic freedom fighter Aung San Suu Kyi, who has staked her life on democracy for her people. Two prisoners-turned-presidents of their countries, South Africa's Nelson Mandela and the Czech Republic's Vaclav Havel, are classic examples of servant leadership. As Havel said, "Hope is not optimism; hope drives us to undertake good deeds, even when the chance of failure is great."

LOOKING BACK, I SEE that my own study of the subject began on a late spring day in 1957 after a short drive from Georgetown to Lexington, Kentucky, to interview with a man who had been my idol for years and was to become my first mentor in leadership.

My high school teammates and I often fantasized about receiving a recruiting call from Adolph Rupp asking if we would like to attend a Wildcats' game in Lexington. Kentucky legends and All-Americans Ralph Beard, "Wah Wah" Jones, and Alex Groza were truly bigger than life. And when Rupp, "The Baron of the Bluegrass," appeared at courtside, the place would go wild. As for playing for Adolph Rupp, well, that would be the ultimate. Of course, that never happened for any of us. But here I was, at age twenty-four, sitting across the desk from the Baron, in the University's Memorial Coliseum, its corridors papered with images of Kentucky All-Americans and championship teams.

"Have a seat," he said in a voice that was a curious mix of relaxed Southern smoothness and crisp military command. He was University of Kentucky Head Basketball Coach Adolph Rupp, the man who had been a hero of mine since I was a kid growing up outside of Louisville, after having moved there from Quicksand in the 1940s.

"Thank you," I replied, as respectfully as I could, and sat

down. I had been practicing what I would say and how I would say it all the way during the eleven-mile, twenty-minute ride over to Lexington from Georgetown where I was teaching and coaching the baseball team at my alma mater, Georgetown College. The early spring air was sweet with the smell of mown grass and damp hay. This was horse country where champions are bred, and competition is a way of life. Winning was in the air, and the scent got stronger as I neared Lexington where Rupp had already established a tradition of championships. My youthful dream—a meeting with Adolph Rupp, a visit to Memorial Coliseum—was now a reality. I was intoxicated, and awed, with the possibilities.

Rupp was looking for an assistant coach and scout, and Harry Lancaster, Rupp's right-hand man, had mentioned me favorably to the Baron. I knew Lancaster as a Georgetown graduate. Once he was seated, Rupp wasted no time getting to the point.

"Can you recruit for me the best basketball players in the world?" he asked, without emotion, the way he would ask somebody to get him a Coke.

"Sir, I certainly will try," I responded.

"Dammit, son!" he barked, leaning forward and driving his elbows into the desktop, his clenched hands seeming as large as bowling balls at the ends of his shirtsleeves. "The last guy *tried*! That's the reason he isn't here!"

"Now I've blown it," I thought. I had stumbled out of the starting gate. But, there was to be another chance.

"Let's start over," Rupp said, leaning back as if to neutralize the air between us. He straightened in his seat and began again.

"Can you recruit the best basketball players in the world?"

"Yes, sir!" I said quickly and confidently. "Yes, sir. No doubt about it. I can and will."

"That's good," he shot back. "I'll be in touch in a day or so."

And that was it. I managed a "Thank you, sir; I'll look forward to hearing from you," as I stood and found my way out the door. The call came a few restless days and nights later. I had the job. Rupp's phone message from Lexington was unambiguous: "Come over here and do what you said you would do."

The salary: $300 per month. The year: April 1957.

AFTER MY VERY formative year with Rupp, I spent the next thirty years in academic leadership, my calling. I was the second leader of a little "start-up" school, Florida Presbyterian College of St. Petersburg, Florida, which blossomed into Eckerd College. Later I was leader of Queens College in Charlotte, North Carolina—an academic "turn-around" school, now thriving as Queens University of Charlotte. In both cases, I was part of a team, and the good things we achieved were achieved as a team. But in both cases I was called to be the leader of the team.

I remember that frightening and exhilarating moment in 1968 when the board of trustees of Florida Presbyterian College asked me to serve as president. It was one of the shortest presidential searches in American higher education history: President Bill Kadel resigned on April 30, and three days later I was standing in the crosshairs. The reason was obvious. The college couldn't afford to wait for an extended search. I knew that well, having served as a tenured professor, coach, dean, and vice president of development since the school's opening in 1960.

It was a daunting challenge—and I was all of thirty-five years old. Admissions for the fall were short of projections; we faced a serious and immediate budget shortfall; and the president and academic dean, extraordinary servant leaders in their own rights, had both resigned, exhausted from the 24/7 demands of starting an ambitious private college that sought "excellence in all things." I believed deeply in the college's innovative, liberal arts mission and recalled vividly the advice Coach Rupp gave me when I left the University of Kentucky: "Billy, I hate to see you go, but best wishes. And, just remember: Winners know how to win. Believe in what you are doing. Have a passion for it. If it was easy, everyone would be doing it. Take on the tough tasks: They will define you."

At that very moment, I had all but accepted another college presidency in Tennessee. That other job would have been far less challenging than assuming the leadership of struggling Florida Presbyterian. But, after reflection on Rupp's counsel and conversations with faculty friends, I said yes to Florida Presbyterian.

Nine years later, saying yes to another struggling academic institution, Queens in Charlotte, wasn't quite the same, but I still had those moments of cold sweat in the middle of the night, wondering, "Am I right for this job?" In the 1970s, Queens was in very big trouble. We had been successful at Eckerd College, and I had become known as an educational innovator. But could I help this little liberal arts college called Queens?

Would I be accepted in comparatively conservative Charlotte? Eckerd had become known as "The Berkeley of the East," not only for its academic distinction, but for its large number of radical students. In the spirit of the times, while I was at Eckerd, black students took over a building and the fashionable campus dress of the era—braless and barefoot—was everywhere evident. There were ceaseless protests against the Vietnam War, against discrimination against women and minorities, and against the cafeteria fare—always the cafeteria fare.

I recall vividly an experience with a bright, young, African American student. Wearing granny glasses and baggy, used Army/Navy store clothes, she came to my office unannounced and in a crisp, clear voice stated her mission: "You are the man. You run this plantation. The black students are not pleased with the number of black faculty, and we want more emphasis on black history in the curriculum. And, we will use 'any means necessary' to right these wrongs."

"Clear enough," I responded. "Will you and your fellow students help us in the process?"

Response: "I am not a fellow; I am a woman." Then she concluded, "We will help if you are serious."

We—and they—were serious, and this young woman went on not only to help with her mission, which we only partially achieved with respect to black faculty, but also to graduate with honors and then to attend law school.

After seventeen years at Eckerd (nine as president), I felt the call to move on; the far horizon beckoned. Queens was obviously a risky choice. Not only was it relatively unknown to me personally, it was also floundering by most objective measures. Friends told me that anyone in his right mind would stick to the known and safe, the predictable future, the beaten path.

Instead, I went to Queens.

In part, I went because I heard the voice of Adolph Rupp: "Take on the tough tasks. They will define you." And, in part, I went because a remarkable man named Bill Lee had entered my life.

BILL LEE WAS SOON to become leader of Duke Power (today, Duke Energy), one of the giants in American energy development, and as a neighbor, Bill Lee had come to love struggling Queens College. Lee turned down an invitation to join the Princeton University board of trustees, because, as he told Princeton's president, "My little Presbyterian college up the street needs me more than Princeton. I am honored, but talk to me later." Servant leadership personified. Lee had carved out endless hours from his exhausting schedule to help Queens gasp for breath, but he knew Queens needed something more than constant resuscitation.

Bill Lee called me at Eckerd from his Charlotte office. Would I consider moving to Charlotte and leading Queens? I was sure that he immediately detected my reluctance. For its part, Queens was a college for women; shouldn't it consider a woman for president? For my part, I was weighing opportunities in a family business, in banking, and even in politics. But, none of these opportunities struck my imagination or stirred my soul. I yearned to stay in academia with its fascinating connection to youth and learning.

I had reviewed Queens's financial position: It was dire but not hopeless, if the college painted quickly with bold strokes.

Lee's message communicated this sense of urgency and was loud, clear, and convincing in another way, too: "Dr. Wireman," he began with that stern moral earnestness characteristic of his Carolina Presbyterian ancestors, "Queens is an institution of your church. You are a Presbyterian elder and have taught church school classes. You have an obligation, indeed a duty, to visit Queens and share with us your impressions. We will send you a ticket. When can you come?"

Given Lee's persuasive powers and the logic of his argument, to paraphrase a great orator, "I came, I saw, and I signed on."

It was clear that Charlotte was on the move and that its business, cultural, and religious communities were supportive and wanted Queens, founded in 1857, to have a bright future. The Belk, Harris, and Barnhardt families, along with other prominent Charlotte citizens, had been strong supporters of the college. Charlotte, a stronghold of Presbyterianism, had no thoughts of letting Queens expire—maybe change or merge, but never die. The task was to restore confidence in its future.

But Queens was in trouble. And I had just spent nine years helping another struggling Presbyterian school turn around and learn to fly.

Lots could go wrong. I could fail. I could be the goat. Staying in Florida would be lots safer.

But, again, I heard Adolph Rupp's voice: "Billy, take on the tough tasks."

And I heard, too, the voice of another great friend and mentor, entrepreneur Jack Eckerd, the king of retail, the man who created the vast chain of drugstores. I could hear Jack say: "Billy, no risk, no gain. It's better to transform, to create something better, than to just transact, just move things around."

And now here was Bill Lee, with his earnest commitment not simply to his career or even his company, but to his community.

So I went to Queens, off on yet another odyssey in leadership.

In 1978, as the new president of Queens, I was making the rounds of influential Charlotteans and members of the board of trustees as I began my tenure, recognizing that the enthusiastic support of the city and its leaders would be essential to any success I might have in my new job.

Hugh McColl was on everyone's list as Charlotte's upcoming power broker, and I knew I had to see him early on.

In 1978, McColl was a man in a fearsome hurry. He was the very able and ambitious heir apparent of North Carolina National Bank (NCNB). He was building a vast banking empire and was crucial to Queens's future. As fate would have it, a key executive on my staff, Joe Martin, was a close ally of McColl, and he helped prepare me for our first encounter. I had heard that McColl was a direct man, rather impatient, not given to small talk or idle gossip, and liked to get right to the point. In the words of one observer, "He believes in winning and takes no prisoners." On the way to the bank, I asked Martin again to pinpoint what we might expect. His answer was clear: "He'll ask you why you came to Queens and what you plan to do to get the college on a sound financial and academic track." I felt as ready as the situation allowed.

Straight off the elevator, we were ushered into McColl's moderately sized office on the twenty-third floor of the NCNB building. Family pictures and mementoes were sprinkled around the room. McColl was sitting behind his desk wearing a rumpled oversized button-down, white shirt and a conservative red tie: his all-business appearance and demeanor bespoke power and high energy. Following a firm handshake, we all sat down. Then he sprang up, began to walk around the room with a bounce, and with palpable aggressiveness, peppered me with rapid-fire questions. I decided then and there that I liked him. Now I must get him to like me.

"You know," he started, "you have to stop the hemorrhaging out there. Can you do that? You know you can't continue to run deficits. What are your plans?" My thoughts returned to Rupp's question two decades earlier.

This time I was more positive and to the point—no more "I'll try."

"I want Queens to combine academic distinction and financial viability," I replied as upbeat as I could. "I see Queens's difficulties as a great opportunity to build a college that can become the jewel in Charlotte's crown [a phrase that Bill Lee used]. We can paint with bold strokes. I did not come here to fail," I concluded, if the truth be known, with more confidence than the reality of the situation justified.

"Fine," he responded sharply.

I was so satisfied with my response, and McColl's reaction to it, that I felt comfortable putting a like question to Mr. McColl. "And what, sir, do you plan to do with this bank?"

"I plan to turn it into the biggest bank in America!" he shot back without hesitation.

"And why is that important?" I asked.

"Because I am tired of having to go hat-in-hand to New

York for money. I want to **serve** our people from here."

McColl's message: I want to **serve first**, then **lead** to more and closer opportunities for my community to secure capital. This was my very first glimpse of Hugh McColl's vision of manifest destiny for Charlotte. And, you know, he never wavered from that combination of building a great bank to **serve** a great community.

A few pleasantries followed. McColl wished me well, and then Joe Martin signaled that it was time to leave. As we were exiting, McColl asked, "Were you in the service?"

"Yes," I responded. "I served as a Marine officer for two years after college."

He broke into a broad smile and proclaimed with a rising voice, "So did I. I got my management training in the Marine Corps." I responded with the Marine Corps motto, "Semper Fi"—always faithful. As we shook hands again, I sensed that I might have passed the first test.

On the way back to Queens, I asked Joe Martin what he thought. "So far, so good," Martin opined, "but the big test will be in what we do. Hugh McColl is a man of action." Over the next two and a half decades, I realized many times the prescience of Martin's description.

Twenty-four years later, on a crisp spring afternoon, Hugh McColl stood at a podium on Queens's front lawn beneath the stately oaks that are a signature of the campus, to speak words of congratulations upon my retirement as president of the college. McColl himself had just recently retired as Chairman and CEO of Bank America, now the largest bank in America, which he had built, as he said he would, over the years since our first meeting. He also had served as chairman of the Queens board of trustees for the past ten years. With his leadership, and that of former chairs Joe Grier, Jimmie Harris, and Bill Lee, we had made great progress toward fulfilling my bold promise from years before. In those years, the college became coed; added more than $30 million in campus improvements; raised enrollment by three hundred percent; increased its endowment tenfold; won four awards from the Council for Advancement and Support of Education (CASE); boasted four North Carolina Professors of the Year; added well-regarded graduate programs in business, education, nursing, communication, and creative writing; was consistently recognized as one of the top Southern universities by *US News & World Report*; and evolved to university status.

In addition to the McColl Graduate School of Business MBA being voted the best in the greater Charlotte area for several years in a row, Dr. Ernie Boyer, president of the Carnegie Foundation for the Advancement of Teaching and former U.S. Secretary of Education, praised Queens's undergraduate program. That program engages all students in a four-year core liberal learning program, involves all students in an internship program (voted number one in America), and provides an international study experience for 90 percent of students through the John Belk International Program (overall, only 10 percent of American college students study abroad annually). Dr. Boyer said, "I know of no college that has combined the four elements as successfully as you have in a curriculum core that has coherence, in an international program that has great vision, in a blending of the liberal and useful arts through an enriched major, and through an internship that tries to relate the classroom to the realities of life."

And, in our spare time, we raised $125 million.

THE SUCCESS OF QUEENS is due in no small part due to the efforts of Hugh McColl and Bill Lee, the many dedicated members of the Queens board, and thousands of concerned Presbyterians, Charlotteans, graduates and other friends. But Adolph Rupp and Jack Eckerd must be credited as well, for these men, my bosses and mentors, shaped my leadership and its effects on Queens.

I have been very fortunate to know these four men and to have worked with and for them. My grandmother Mary's advice had taken root: I had "associated with capable people" and thus had been in the position to learn from Rupp, Eckerd, Lee, and McColl. They have been the big guys in my life, and the leadership methods I have learned from them have been of immeasurable value to me and to those I influenced in return. By working with these giants at critical points in their own professional journeys on the way to the top, I learned key lessons about life and leadership.

The success I've had as a leader has been due in no small measure to the teachers I had. I was blessed to have four remarkable mentors who were astonishingly effective leaders. And now I'd like to teach you something of what they taught me, not to demonstrate my own wisdom but to demonstrate theirs.

That's why this book is not exactly about me. Yet, it's not only about them. Heaven knows, each was a fascinating person, and their life stories are the stuff of high adventure, but in what follows, I'm not trying to tell their life stories. What I want to share is what they taught me about servant leadership.

I want to tell you about the themes, the principles, the lessons, and the visions they taught me, those "winged horses that never tire" that carried me through my odyssey in servant leadership and can carry you through yours.

The fuel of that odyssey is hope; that's why I'm so fond of Robert Louis Stevenson's remark that "to travel hopefully is a better thing than to arrive." Leadership has everything to do with character and ultimately with spirit; it has to do in the end not with getting and spending and career advancement, but with growing as a person, as a citizen, as a spiritual being. That's why I'm fond of another Stevenson observation (from his *Familiar Studies of Men and Books*): "To be what we are, and to become what we are capable of becoming, is the only end of life."

While each of my mentors was unique in his own right, collectively they represent both the motto of Queens University of Charlotte as well as the pragmatic imperative of Servant Leadership: "Not to be served, but to serve."

Let's now turn to the experience I shared with each of my teachers.

A young Billy Wireman with Adolph Rupp, 1957.

Adolph Rupp:
Baron of the Bluegrass

"He thought that when a Kentucky baby boy was born, the mother had two wishes for him: to grow up to be like another native son, Abraham Lincoln, and to play basketball for Adolph Rupp."

—Russell Rice
Adolph Rupp biographer

"Coach Rupp knew how to sharpen iron with iron."

—Jim Dinwiddle
Kentucky basketball player, 1969-71

There are many who would never think of Adolph Rupp as a servant leader. But those who look beyond the rough surface and sometimes harsh manner will learn that everything Rupp did was calculated to lead his teams to victory and his players to personal success. That is, in my view, the epitome of the servant leader, and it was a vital part of Rupp's winning tradition.

I began discovering this essential truth about Adolph Rupp during my very first meeting with him. It was neither auspicious nor one that boded well for my future with the most successful and revered basketball coach of the era. At the time, I was a sophomore guard on the Georgetown College basketball team coached by Humsey Yessin, Rupp's former team manager at Kentucky. Georgetown was only eleven miles from Lexington and several times that year before the 1951-52 season opened, we scrimmaged Kentucky at Memorial Coliseum in Lexington. Rupp saw this as opportunity to test his Wildcats against relatively weak, nonthreatening opposition to iron out the kinks for another NCAA Championship, which he had won in 1951, his third, following titles in 1948 and 1949 with the celebrated "Fabulous Five."

Being a Rupp protege, Yessin had naturally installed the Kentucky system at Georgetown. The basic Kentucky play was a "second guard around." The first guard would pass to the forward and go inside. The forward would dribble toward the center, pivot, and hand off to the second guard who would then go in for a lay-up. Simple enough. It was Kentucky's bread and butter play. Both teams knew it by heart. On this particular occasion, I was paired with a lanky, 6'3" future All-American Frank Ramsey. I was all of 5'8".

After bringing the ball up-court, we moved into the basic play. It unfolded flawlessly. The first guard to the forward, the forward dribbled to the center, pivoted, and handed off to me, the second guard. Ramsey got caught in the pick, and I went in for a perfect by-the-book "bunny" lay-up. "Wow," I said to myself, "not bad for a scrawny 5'8" kid from Quicksand."

A shrill whistle shattered my sense of joy. Activity came to a dead stop. A feather falling would have shattered the silence. Then, Rupp began to speak. Ramsey stood at limp, rapt attention. A stony hush filled the cavernous Memorial Coliseum. I noticed Kentucky All-American Cliff Hagan, shoulders drooped, gazing up at the eleven thousand empty seats as if to say, "Okay, here it comes; we've heard it before."

And indeed, it came. The forty players, coaches and managers stood in eerie silence as Rupp critiqued what had just happened to one of Kentucky's future all-time greats. "Frank," he began in a sarcastic, high-pitched Kansas twang, "see that little piece of horse manure [Rupp used an earthier term] over there?" pointing menacingly at me. "He just went by you so fast that you caught pneumonia in the right lung. Not only did he score, but now the University will have to pay your doctor bill. If you want to watch the game, Frank, buy a ticket and sit in the stands. Eat popcorn and drink Cokes with your girlfriend. Here, on the court, Frank, you are expected to be a player, not a spectator." The scrimmage ended shortly thereafter, and I avoided Ramsey deliberately because he was not in the mood to chat. He did, however, go on to earn All-American honors, join the Boston Celtics as the best "sixth man" in basketball, and then be inducted into the Basketball Hall of Fame. I left the Coliseum a little proud of myself, walking down the corridors that had seen so many All-Americans and championship teams walking confidently from the locker room to the court where victory was usually assured. I had momentarily been a part of that storied history, but I had no inkling of what was to come.

Fast-forward to Lexington, Kentucky, on March 24, 1958, the highest moment in the life of America's most famous basketball coach. As fate would have it, I had a front-row seat: two nights earlier Adolph Rupp had won the NCAA championship, his fourth at the University of Kentucky. At the time, Rupp held the record for NCAA basketball championships.

A bright spring sun bathed Memorial Coliseum. Inside, a wildly appreciative overflow crowd rejoiced with a warm, palpable, prideful glee. I was keenly aware that the past season had been a miracle, like my having the opportunity to coach with Adolph Rupp. During that memorable year, as Rupp's assistant, I had scouted opponents, helped with the freshman team, driven him to numerous speaking engagements, and spent many hours walking on his beloved bluegrass farm in central Kentucky where he raised Hereford cattle. While on the farm, I listened to his reflections on family, basketball, politics, and sundry other topics.

I assumed Coach Rupp considered it a miracle season, too. Kentucky was not supposed to win the national championship this year. The players were too small and too erratic. But there we were, together, celebrating a happy occasion—the winningest coach in basketball, now with four national championships, and a novice assistant filled with awe and respect. The entire state was busting with pride, and Rupp was the reason. The famous bluegrass in central Kentucky was said to stand at appreciative attention. In your mind's eye you could see the thoroughbred racehorses at famous Calumet Farm outside Lexington as they pawed at the floor in their immaculately clean white stalls, rearing their heads with lusty "I-told-you-so" snorts.

As we walked from the locker room corridor to the waiting roaring crowd, I asked, hoping to get a jewel or two to use in my future coaching career, "Coach, you must be very proud today. This team was not picked by anyone to win." He nodded approvingly. "Is there anything you did special this year?"

His response, again in that deep Kansas twang, was quick, to the point, and applicable far beyond basketball: "Billy, there was nothing special. You just concentrate on the fundamentals, and the rest will take care of itself. There are no shortcuts to success. In basketball, as in life, if you get the fundamentals right, over the long haul, you will win more than you lose, and occasionally you experience a pleasant surprise." A pleasant surprise? The National Championship!

Get the fundamentals right. If you focus on the fundamentals, you can be a master of the game. And if ever one was a "master of the game" it was Adolph Rupp. How this remarkable man, who would likely have been a success in any field he chose, turned Kentucky into a hotbed of basketball respected throughout the world, is a story that has been told before and still offers many valuable lessons for us today. Rupp has been called "The George Patton of Basketball," and his story is rooted firmly in Americana.

The year was 1930, America was deep in the Great Depression, and the University of Kentucky was looking for a basketball coach. In the eighteen years from 1912 to 1930, eight different coaches had guided the Wildcats to so-so seasons. The last Kentucky coach during this period, John Mauer, who had played football at the University of Illinois with the legendary "Red" Grange, resigned because Kentucky would not give him a raise despite his three-year, 40-16 record.

Meanwhile, at Freeport High School in Illinois, a young Kansas University graduate, Adolph Rupp, was compiling an impressive four-year, 59-21 record. Rupp had played basketball under the famed Dr. Forrest "Phog" Allen and developed a friendship with former Kansas coach, Dr. James Naismith, who invented basketball at the Springfield, Massachusetts, YMCA in 1892. In 1922, Rupp played on Allen's national championship team.

University of Illinois Head Basketball Coach Craig Ruby was impressed with Rupp's coaching style. Because of his record, Rupp was a hot college coaching prospect, but he wasn't sure he wanted to stay in coaching. He believed he could make more money in school administration. After all, he was graduated Phi Beta Kappa from Kansas in 1923 with majors in economics and history. And in the spring of 1930, he received his master's degree in education from Columbia University in New York. Not bad for a second-generation German immigrant who spoke no English until he was nine years old. But, when highly respected Craig Ruby recommended him to Kentucky officials, Rupp decided to take a look.

And he signed on. Then for the next forty-two years, from 1930 to 1972, Adolph Frederick Rupp compiled a record that ranks with the all-time greats in any sport: four national champions, twenty-seven Southeastern Conference titles, ten consensus All-Americans, one Olympic championship, one National Invitation Tournament championship, and five Hall of Fame members, including himself. For eighteen years, he held the record for national titles, until being deposed by UCLA's John Wooden in the seventies and early eighties. For twenty-five years, he owned the record for most victories, 876. North Carolina's Dean Smith passed him in total victories in 1997. Kentucky still holds the record for most team victories.

Rupp built this winning tradition because he taught his players to master the fundamentals of the game. He expected his coaches to master the fundamentals of their jobs, too. I reported to work for what was to become an all too brief, but memorable year on August 1, 1957. My duties were outlined in a meeting with Coach Rupp and longtime assistant Harry Lancaster shortly after arrival: scout Kentucky opponents Temple, SMU, and West Virginia, all before December 15. I was to report for all practices while in town dressed in the company uniform: starched khakis, tennis shoes, and a whistle, even though I had no instructions on when to use the latter. Lancaster told me later that while we all had whistles, only one was to be used during practice—Rupp's. I also was to help with the freshmen team and scan a dozen or so sports pages throughout Kentucky to monitor how hot-shot prospective Wildcats were doing. During the season, on nights when Kentucky wasn't playing, I was to scout Kentucky's most promising high school prospects and report regularly to Rupp and Lancaster. Coach Rupp prepared for the basketball season the way a general prepares for battle, and he expected his lieutenants to be on their toes.

Each practice looked and sounded a lot like boot camp. The first day set the tone for the year: At 3:30 P.M., with the only sound the monotonous bounce of basketballs, Rupp blew his whistle and called the team to center court. I can still see us there today: Rupp, Lancaster, and Wireman, the new recruit.

Rupp broke the silence. "Well 'booyees'," he announced with that Kansas twang, "it's time to begin preparation for the National Championship. This is all business, and it will take a great coaching job to win the title with you guys. You know the rules: speak only when you can improve the silence, and remember the importance of fundamentals: protecting the ball, blocking out on rebounds, no turnovers, passing to the lead man. We will win by hard work, defense, sticking to our knitting and believing in ourselves. Harry, anything else?" Harry had nothing to add, except a brief introduction of me. Rupp blew his whistle with, "Let's go to work."

The 105-minute practice sessions began with open shooting for thirty minutes, two men to a ball. Then lay-ups. Then followed drills, drills, and more drills (passing and screening, blocking out, and the basic offense), free throw shooting, and then wind sprints. At 5:15 P.M., Rupp's whistle signaled the end of the session, and the players quietly walked off the court to shower and dress. The coaches retired to the coach's dressing room. Again, with little, if any, conversation. With the exception of reviewing a scouting report for an upcoming opponent and scrimmaging more as the season wore on, this was the pattern of every practice.

The players didn't see it, and perhaps I didn't at the time, but what Coach Rupp was doing with these monotonous drills was building their self-confidence. Therein lies Rupp's main claim to servant leadership. Time and again, in talking with former Rupp players, they commented on the fact that, while they didn't like it at the time, they felt that the drive for perfection and development of self-confidence were indelible legacies of Rupp's coaching and leadership style.

Run the drill until you get it right. Run it some more until you have it perfectly. When the players have confidence that the play will work, like the famous "second guard around" play, the many shifting contexts and situations of the actual game are not worrisome. If you rely on the fundamental skills, acquired through hard practice, you will always have confidence that they will see you through the most trying of circumstances—when the game is on the line. Rupp's practice sessions were intended to make his players masters of the game.

Frank Deford caught the essence of this strategy in a *Sports Illustrated* story on Rupp: "It seems that Rupp, who has never been encumbered by modesty, used to teach a basketball course at UK, and he would always give all of his students A's. Rupp's reasoning was simply that no one could learn basketball from Adolph Rupp and not get an A."

Adolph Rupp definitely liked the spotlight, and the bigger the arena the better. He often asked recruits if they wanted to play in Carnegie Hall or the Cow Palace. Rupp liked playing a "Carnegie Hall schedule," and he knew it would draw players who liked to compete with the best and for high stakes. Of course, in Rupp's opinion, other than Madison Square Garden, Lexington's Memorial Coliseum was the nation's showcase for basketball talent. By the late 1940s, every Kentucky lad, and many from out of state, wanted to play for Rupp in Lexington, which became, in Al McGuire's words, "the only true capital of basketball" (*Wisdom*, p. 36).

In 1930, when Rupp arrived for his job interview at Kentucky, the encounter would reveal a key element of his success over the years—his public confidence in his abilities. Arriving dressed to the nines for the interview, he reminded one committee member of a preacher with smartly parted hair and spit-polished black shoes. Immediately into the interview, Rupp made it clear that he did not want a contract, either long or short. If he produced, they would keep him. If he didn't, they could fire him. If he wanted to move on, he would just go. No messy negotiations. One committee member asked him why the University should hire him; he was relatively young—twenty-nine—and had no previous college coaching experience. His quick answer has become part of his legend and convinced the committee to select him over seventy candidates: "Winners know how to win," he said. "And I am a winner." "Besides," he concluded, "I am the best damned basketball coach in America."

And that's exactly what he proved to be. Rupp's self-confident boast is a classic example of the bravado exhibited by ancient warriors like Achilles and Beowulf. It is not enough for the truly heroic to exude self-confidence. Such heroes also must make it public, go out on a limb by boasting of deeds to come, and then make good on the promise. The brag of excellence is not as common today as it was in the heroic age; but we must remember that if you can do it, it's not bragging! Men such as Rupp do not wait for others to set the standards they will meet; they set the bar high for themselves and then prove true to their word. Self-effacing humility was not a virtue of the heroic age. Nor was selfish pride. Neither was in Rupp's arsenal, but courage and self-confidence were. And these led to the success he promised.

He took the Kentucky job on approval, making it easy for university officials to remove him if he did not produce, which of course put more pressure on him. For Rupp, the pressure generated success. He finally accepted a contract in 1947 after he had won more than three hundred games, nine SEC Championships, and an NIT Title.

Rupp thrived in the competitive and very public arena of

college basketball. And so did his players. Rupp felt very strongly about the competitive nature of sport, disagreeing with Grantland Rice's statement that "it matters not if you won or lost, but how you played the game." Rupp's view was, "If it doesn't make any difference, why put scoreboards up there? Why keep score? Why, it makes all the difference in the world. I don't believe I've held my job here at the University with the idea in mind that our alumni and our student body don't care whether we won or lost around here" (Cawood Ledford, *Funny Things Happen*, p. 53). To this he added, "I'm not engaged in a popularity contest. I want to win basketball games."

Rupp saw competitiveness in a broad context. In a letter to Bill Myers in 1965, he wrote, "To be successful, a coach must create within his boys a competitive spirit that will bring success. In our free enterprise system, we should encourage competition" (quoted in Rice, p. 211). In an earlier letter to John Burt, the personnel director of National Basketball Inter-collegiate Coaching Organization, in 1961, Rupp laid it on the line: "I would not care to live in a society unless it be competi-tive. I think our sports teach that better than most other phases of education" (Rice, p. 217).

Rupp's competitive nature was not limited to the hard-woods. During one of our weekly coaches' meetings where we analyzed who was looking good in practice, the players' grades, and who needed work, Rupp and Lancaster had an interesting exchange. Last Saturday, Rupp informed us, one of his prized Hereford calves had won a blue ribbon in a fat cattle show. He went in to great detail to extol the virtues of her shiny orange coat, her pretty blue eyes, her rounded, near perfect rump.

When he finished, Lancaster said to Rupp, "Adolph, I believe you like that calf better than you like Esther" [Rupp's wife]. Rupp's quick response: "Why, hell, yes. What did she ever win?"

It was important for Rupp to build this competitive spirit in his players. On the one hand, there was the school's winning tradition that each player had to live up to. Rupp never let them forget that. It loomed over them like Rupp's own giant frame and powerful countenance. It was something for them to build on, but also something they, like Rupp, did not want to let down.

But a grand winning tradition was not itself, in Rupp's mind, enough to ensure that each player achieved more than even he thought he was capable of. Rupp would challenge each player to exceed his own estimation of himself, his own best effort—another example of servant leadership. Kentucky All-American Ralph Beard said it well: "He would not accept defeat, and he didn't want anybody who played for him to accept defeat. And it always killed him, as it did us" (*Wisdom*, p. 82).

One way Rupp pushed his players was to embarrass them with sarcasm. As team physician Dr. V. A. Jackson has observed, Rupp "was a master psychologist which I am sure is one big reason he was such a great coach. He seemed always to know just what to say to a player and how to say it in order to make the player try harder" (*Beyond the Baron*, p. 9). Jackson recalls a player once telling him, "Doctor, at times he makes you so mad you actually hate him, and you think, you old son-of-a-bitch, I'll show you I can play basketball, and you go out there and play your heart out" (*Beyond the Baron*, p. 125).

Kentucky's All-American 6'3" guard Frank Ramsey (1951-54) said it most succinctly: "He convinced us we could do things we didn't know we could do" (*Wisdom*, p. 26). Getting the very best performance out of your troops is the highest calling of any leader—particularly servant leaders.

Examples of his motivational sarcasm are legion. On one occasion he told All-American Bill Spivey, after a particularly flatfooted play by the 7'1" center, "Bill, we now have a wonderful new invention. There is a camera that can take your picture moving. So, you don't have to stand in the same place all the time." When the team's academic achievement left something to be desired, Rupp commented, "I'm afraid when they pass out the Phi Beta Kappa keys this year, there won't be many dangling from our boys' watch chains" (*Funny Things*, p. 99). When the entire team's play disappointed him, he could say things like, "They're like a bunch of quails: somebody shoots, and they all scatter."

Defeating a vastly outmanned Arkansas State team 34-4 at halftime in the 1944–45 season, Rupp noticed that the four points were all made by the same player, number 12. "Who's guarding number 12?" Rupp demanded in the locker room. All-American Jack Parkinson raised his hand, and Rupp growled, "Well, get on him! Your man is going wild." (*Funny Things*, p. 58-59). When the 1958 team played poorly against a weak Loyola team, Rupp didn't go into the locker room with the team at the half. Rather, he stuck his head in just before the second half began and said, "Oh, excuse me, I didn't know this was the ladies' room" (Jackson, pp. 65-66). Here are a few others:

- To Milt Ticco after he missed an easy shot that would

have tied Ohio State: "The Buckeyes ought to be awarding you a varsity letter."

• To Tommy Kron: "Did you know I'm writing a book entitled 'What Not to Do in Basketball'? The first 200 pages are about you."

• To John Crigler: "John, 150 years from now there will be no university, no field house. There will have been an atomic war, and it will all be destroyed. Underneath the rubble will be a monument, on which is the inscription, Here lies John Crigler, the most stupid basketball player ever at Kentucky. Killed by Adolph Rupp."

• To Ernest Sparkman during the 1944 NIT: "Sparkman, you see that center circle? I want you to go out there and take a crap. Then you can go back to Carr Creek and tell them you did something in Madison Square Garden."

• To Vernon Hatton after Hatton asked for the game ball from the December 7, 1957, Temple game: "Give you the game ball? Just because you scored two points from forty-seven feet with one second to go, you want me to give you the game ball? How would I explain that to the Athletics Board, giving away a thirty-five dollar basketball?" Rupp finally gave Hatton the ball, but he wanted him to earn it "psychologically" as well as on the court.

• On the 1957–58 team: "They're not the greatest basketball players in the world, all they can do is win. They're not concert violinists, but they sure can fiddle." This team became known as the "Fiddling Five," and they won the National Championship in my year with Rupp.

But Rupp could also show a lighter side, especially with friends and when he was the subject: His longtime friend,

Kentucky Governor "Happy" Chandler once asked him if they should salute him at his funeral with a strong shot of Kentucky Bourbon whiskey on the way to the cemetery or on the way back. "Governor," he responded, "let's do it on the way in. I won't be with you on the way back."

Rupp's love of the public spotlight is evident in the way he managed the press. He was always good copy, and he became a celebrity, perhaps the first basketball coach to become an icon of the game. He was an imposing man who created a commanding presence when he entered a room, especially if it was filled with sports reporters. Then his elfish wit would flash.

When asked how his 1953–54 team managed to go undefeated, he replied, "Superior coaching." When asked after losing a game, "Hey, Coach, what went wrong?" he groused, "Don't call me coach. A team that only scores twelve points in the second half doesn't have a coach."

There is more than a hint of irony in these remarks. In fact, their intentions might be reversed. Could we read "superior coaching" for "the team did it," and could the second statement really mean it was the coach, and not the team, that was responsible for a poor performance in the second half? Only Coach Rupp knew for sure. As C. Ray Hall once observed, Coach Rupp "was not only an iconic presence, but an ironic one. He could be in the action, and above it" (*Wisdom*, p. 68).

Rupp dominated the game during the era of segregation, and he was accused by some of being a racist. Over the years I have been asked dozens of times if Rupp had a prejudiced attitude toward African-Americans. My response is always the same: I spent literally dozens of hours alone with Rupp on speaking and scouting trips and walking with him on his farm.

I never asked, and the subject of race never came up, and we covered virtually every subject in the human experience. If he was prejudiced toward anyone other than basketball referees, I never heard it mentioned.

Rupp was a well-read and well-informed man, having earned a master's degree in education from Columbia University. He often used his background, especially his familiarity with the Bible, in his barbs. He was known for recruiting kids from the Kentucky hills, which had a special place in his heart, as confirmed by his frequent quoting of the verse: "I will lift up mine eyes to the hills, whence cometh my help" (Psalms, 121:1). After a road game in which many of the referees' calls seemed to go against him, Rupp complained to the media about the men in striped shirts by paraphrasing the Bible this way: "I was a stranger, and they took me in."

Clearly, Adolph Rupp enjoyed the spotlight and the arena where he could put his plans into action and his promises of victory on the line. For Rupp, success in the sporting arena was a way of demonstrating personal excellence, achieving one's personal goals and the goals of the team. Keeping score and winning were Rupp's way of measuring his own success and that of his players. He built individual confidence, team confidence, and a winning tradition that perpetuated itself—surely necessary ingredients in leadership.

Rupp loved to build things, too. What he built were championship teams and a winning tradition in Kentucky basketball. By the time he retired in 1972, he had 879 wins with only one hundred and ninety losses (82.2 percent); four NCAA championships (1948, 1949, 1951, 1958); a National Invitational Title (1946); an Olympic title (1948); twenty-seven SEC titles; twenty NCAA tournament appearances; and five Sugar Bowl Tournament championships. He had been named National Coach of the Year two times (1959, 1966); SEC Coach of the Year seven times; and had coached twenty-three All-Americans and twenty-eight players who made it to the professional ranks.

"The tradition of the UK program," says author Lonnie Wheeler, "obviously contributes to the culture, carrying with it a way-back, ancestral aspect" (*Wisdom*, p. 39). Al McGuire adds, "I have touched all the so-called capitals of basketball, but when it gets down to the short stroke, the only true capital of basketball is Lexington. I even think that there are times when the horses kinda bend down a little to the roundball. At Kentucky, basketball is a type of religion, such a fanatical obsession that they expect to be national champions each year." Rupp was the creator and high priest of this religion.

The statistics speak for themselves, but Rupp was more than a list of accomplishments that bespeak a winning tradition. Rupp *was* the tradition. Writing in *Sports Illustrated* in 1966 (March 7), Frank Deford observes with his usual urbanity, "A governor cannot succeed himself in the Commonwealth of Kentucky, and a horse can run only once in the Kentucky Derby, but as long as Adolph Rupp is around, the Bluegrass will never suffer from a lack of continuity. For thirty-six years, in a land of colonels, he has been the only Baron, a man of consummate pride and well-earned privilege . . . he continues to pursue the only challenge left—trying to top himself. And that is some tough act to follow."

Rupp was well respected by his fellow coaches, and admired for what he gave to the game. He introduced the fast break and accelerated the game when there was no shot clock. His focus on fundamentals, set plays, and sound defense produced scores in the hundreds and tremendous winning margins that were impressive to fans and terrifying for the opposition. "He was one of the soundest coaches basketball has ever seen," former UCLA coach John Wooden once said. "He didn't use a lot of fanciness and flair. He didn't need to." Many consider Rupp the best offensive coach and Hank Iba (Oklahoma State) the best defensive coach the game has known, but Rupp stressed defense as well. Once when a fan complained and suggested Rupp should remove one of his players from a game because he was not scoring, Rupp growled, "Neither has the man he's guarding."

Rupp brought big-time basketball to the South and made Kentucky known throughout the nation for its prowess in the sport. "He should be credited with basketball's growth, not just in the South but all over the country in the 1940s and '50s," says Cliff Hagan, a former Kentucky All-American and later the school's athletics director. "Every time you see a basketball goal on a barn or kids in a playground, you have to credit Coach Rupp. His presence will last forever, in Kentucky and nationally." Rupp's real arena was his adopted state. By giving Kentucky, a relatively poor state, a sense of pride, he inspired countless Kentuckians to walk with their heads high.

Adolph Rupp made improvements in the game he loved and built a legacy of champions at Kentucky. He also built pride. Rupp's accomplishments, his legacy, and his vision, were wider than himself, wider than his players and the team, wider even than the University of Kentucky. If you lived in Kentucky in those days, you knew this intuitively. I can remember when I first became aware of the Rupp mystique. When I was in the sixth grade, my class was given a research project on Kentucky's major sources of income. We identified coal, tobacco, horse racing, and whiskey. Our teacher was a Bible belt "teetotaler" and he pointed out that all except coal were "wages of sin."

Next, we were asked to name Kentucky's most famous individuals from history. When we voted on Abraham Lincoln, Jefferson Davis, Henry Clay, and Daniel Boone; Lincoln won hands down. One student protested that Lincoln was a Yankee and was responsible for defeating the South. Then one intrepid young man raised his hand and added his voice to the objection. He said, "We may depend on the 'wages of sin' for our incomes and maybe the Yankees did win the war. But we have Adolph Rupp and Kentucky basketball, and they make us all proud." That pretty much sums it up. If a person can make you feel proud, he or she is both a teacher and a leader.

Rupp's interests and influence extended far beyond the borders of the Bluegrass State and of America. He conducted more overseas clinics than any other coach, including seven in Europe, three in the Far East, and one in the Middle East. He was both a student and a missionary of the game. Representing his country with five of his players at the 1948 Olympic Games where they won the gold medal remained one of Rupp's most heartfelt memories. "My greatest thrill," he once said, "had to be that Olympic team when the kids stood up there in Wembley Stadium and got their gold medals" (*Wisdom*, p. 109).

Rupp's every action, his every comment to an adoring press, his every witticism, and every speech at a banquet over barbecue or fried fish indicated his awareness of the place he occupied in the collective consciousness of Kentucky and the world of basketball. He was aware of the past he had largely created for the basketball program at Kentucky, and he was aware of his role in the context of the present. Ed Beck, who played for Rupp from 1956–58, observed that the coach also "had the ability to look into the future and decide what to do. He made a decision, started at the beginning, and worked toward his goals" (*Wisdom*, p. 69).

This "contextual awareness" contributed to Rupp's success as a coach. He knew that one had to work with the material given him. This is true of every enterprise. Timing and opportunity are necessary ingredients for success. Rupp knew the limitations of his material, and he knew how to create formulas for success. In a letter to Jim Ausenbaugh in 1961, Rupp wrote, "The test of a good coach is if he can win with good material. There are many coaches in the U.S. who have excellent material but just simply don't seem to be able to put over the clincher games. A good coach is the coach who can win when he has the material. It is very seldom that you can take indifferent material and develop it into a championship team" (Rice, p. 214). Although Rupp did just this with his 1958 team, it is significant to note that he recognized the limitations of coaching. Recruiting the good material and being able to recognize it and plan for the future are good evidence of Rupp's contextual thinking. Preparation like this is all in the details as I found out in the fall of 1957.

That fall I was assigned to scout arch-rival West Virginia when they played in Chapel Hill. On the schedule, Carolina was to play the Mountaineers at night. But when I arrived in

Chapel Hill and took a cab to my hotel, I saw fans exiting from where the game was to be played—the game had been changed to the afternoon to accommodate television. You can imagine my nervousness in telling Adolph Rupp that I missed scouting one of our most important opponents because the game was played early. "Billy," he said in an un-fatherly way, "you should have checked it out. That was too important to be left to chance." You can bet that I was especially careful about confirming times and places—sometimes to a fault—in my career from then on. Thankfully, we won the game without a scouting report.

A most important context for Rupp was the community in which he lived. He stayed with one institution most of his professional life and carried the burden of the university's athletic reputation on his back for most of that time. Beyond the university, the community of Lexington, Kentucky, was dear to him. He believed in "giving back," and he was selfless with his time as chairman of the Shriners Hospital for Crippled Children. Rupp was a bear of a man with a steely exterior, but he had a soft side that was rarely visible to those who were not close to him. He would become almost weepy when talking about the plight of children afflicted with polio and other crippling ailments. He was a "Patton on the basketball floor," but, according to his son Herky, "He was a very kindhearted and good father. His image and demeanor on the floor were entirely different than they were at home" (*Wisdom*, p. 70).

Rupp was a complex man. According to Herky Rupp, "He was involved in many, many things. He wasn't a one-dimensional person. He was a three-, four- or five-dimensional person" (*Wisdom*, p. 71).

Above all, he was a teacher. The main way one "gives back" is by "passing on," transmitting the information, the life lessons, the meanings one has uncovered, to the next generation. Rupp did this every day with his players. There were fundamentals, sure, and plays to learn, and skills to acquire. But, there were also life lessons in self-confidence, the rewards of hard work, preparation, and discipline, teamwork, strategy, and the value of competition. He cajoled, criticized, cursed, and connived to get the players' attention and drive them to excellence. "Whatever you do," he said to me one time, "always strive to be the best. And always remember that winners know how to win."

His was not the easy way. You had to sacrifice to play for Rupp, and that in itself was a good lesson. His players have had different reactions to the experience. Vernon Hatton, the player who had trouble prying that game ball from Rupp, said, "It takes six or eight years to get over playing for Coach Rupp. Once you get over it, you get to like him" (*Wisdom*, p. 74). Dan Issel observed, "Coach Rupp could be mean, but not mean-spirited. It's just that he was very disciplined. Most coaches kick you in the butt one minute and pat you on the back the next. Rupp just kicked you in the butt all the time." Some players might have wanted to kill him at times, and almost all were intimidated by him, while some, like Ralph Beard were fiercely loyal: "Some guys say they hated Rupp. Not me. He was it as far as I was concerned. If he told me to run through a brick wall, I'd have backed up as far as it would take" (*Wisdom*, p. 74). Claude Vaughn adds: "He was a very well-educated man. He had a great knowledge of history, and we had more intellectual discussions than anything" (*Wisdom*, p.

72).

But, in the end, all of Rupp's players were driven to play better than they thought they could, on teams that often did better than expected. Rupp lived up to his end of the bargain— if he had good material he would "get over the clincher" and win. There is that fine line in competitive sport between success and triumph. Only the great coaches win consistently even when they have good material.

As I mentioned, one aspect of that complex character was the sarcasm he used as a motivational tool. I came to see that his biting humor was used to keep the players in their place. Rupp constantly distanced himself from his players; he was both in the action and above it. He would immerse himself in the details of a particular game, in a particular season, but his was a wider vision. He was tuned into THE GAME in its larger context and to the tradition of which any particular game was a part. To honor THE GAME and to be true to that tradition, he had to establish his authority and remain in control. Put simply, he viewed things from a different perspective than did his players. Why the distancing? Rupp explained to me one time that it was essential to keep control of every situation. Once when we were walking around his farm on a game day, in khakis of course, I asked him what was the hardest lesson he had to learn as a coach. He then shared an experience that he had as a young coach at Freeport. It seems that a star player's father had challenged him over a disciplinary decision he had made. It was tough, because without this player his team would be weakened considerably. But he stuck to his guns and things came out fine. Then he shared the lesson: "Billy, either you will run your job or it will run you. And don't ever let one of your players get bigger than you. The coach has to have unquestioned authority. If you are not respected, you are finished."

From the beginning in the summer of 1957 to the end of that championship year in the spring of 1958, I learned many valuable lessons from Adolph Rupp that I applied in my later life. There were two particular occasions when his final lesson helped me in my career: When I was the president of Eckerd College in St. Petersburg, I had a senior officer who was considerably older and more experienced than I. This gentleman liked to talk and word came to me that he was bad-mouthing some of my decisions. I remembered Coach Rupp's advice and took steps to remove him, exercising as much courtesy and academic protocol as I could muster. Morale at the college improved considerably, and many trustees and faculty told me later that I had done the right thing.

The other occasion was during my Queens presidency when one of my vice presidents thought he had all the answers about solving the financial challenges we faced. Those were tough days, and we needed all the help we could get. In contrast to the Eckerd situation, this individual had some support in the trustees. Nonetheless, I moved quickly to replace the individual, and again, the situation improved immediately. In these two situations, it was clear that if I didn't run things, they would run me. And if I let either of these gentlemen appear to be dictating to me, then my authority would have been hurt. The lesson here is quintessentially Rupp: The first fundamental of leadership is to be responsible for running the organization. Often I heard him say, "Didn't the Lord in Genesis charge us with dominion?" My grandmother put it another way: One house, one roof, one woman.

Though my time with Rupp was short, the leadership lessons I learned were long-lasting. Rupp was much misunderstood and few saw his human side. His successor, Joe B. Hall, who won the NCAA championship in 1978, and I were inducted into the Alumni Hall of Fame of the University of Kentucky's College of Education in 2001. At the event I asked Joe, who played for Rupp and then served as his assistant before succeeding him as head coach, what he thought of Rupp. His answer is insightful: "Adolph Rupp had a rough exterior that he would like for you to think was the real man. But, it wasn't. Inside was a kind, good, big-hearted man who inspired thousands of players and fans to new heights. All he ever wanted was for each of us to do our best." And that, in the final analysis, is the best that a great servant leader can hope for himself.

Jack Eckerd and Billy Wireman, 1972.

2

Jack Eckerd:
The King of Retail

"It was not enough for Eckerd to simply make money. He put it to work raising a kingdom full of larger-than-life accomplishments."

—The Tampa Tribune

"Jack Eckerd helped pioneer an aggressive brand of marketing that put the word 'entrepreneur' into the American vocabulary."

—Charles Paul Conn
Eckerd biographer

From the campus of Florida Presbyterian College in southern St. Petersburg to Jack Eckerd's office in Clearwater in mid 1968 was a short fifteen-mile, twenty-five-minute drive, straight up U.S. Highway 19. But that short trip could take me, and more importantly, my college, a very long way. I was the freshly installed president of Florida Presbyterian, a start-up school, already acknowledged nationally as one of America's most promising and innovative colleges. Like many start-ups, it was long on innovation and short on cash. I hoped Jack

Eckerd could help me with that. Eckerd, in those days already one of Florida's best-known businessmen, was a college trustee. My first meeting with him after my election as president a month earlier reflected the college's somber mood.

Time in 1966 had described Florida Presbyterian as coming "from vacant lot to excellent in six short years." But growing pains and hard times had hit. Income had not risen as fast as expenses. Utilities, for example, skyrocketed during this period from $200,000 a year to $600,000. In the early sixties, we had proudly built America's first all-electric campus with year-round air-conditioning; thus, the buildings had no windows that would open. My job was to keep the electric bill paid and to save the college from rising debt.

I had assumed the presidency on May 3, 1968, following the former president's resignation on April 30. The college faced a $606,000 deficit in sixty days and was one hundred students short of projected enrollment for the fall. Everyone at Florida Presbyterian knew what had to happen. We had a desperate hunger for short-term cash, but to continue the college's mission we needed some $10 million. And everyone knew that the only person connected with the college who could possibly provide that level of support was Jack Eckerd. If Eckerd agreed to help Florida Presbyterian, the college and all its dreams (not to mention its jobs), could flourish; if he declined, the dreams, and jobs, would die.

Would he help?

At least he had agreed to speak with me.

"Billy," Eckerd said sternly, "you have inherited a tough situation down there. And while you didn't create it, you are the one who is going to have to deal with it. The college is overbuilt and undercapitalized. And the liberal bent of the faculty and students is turning a lot of people off."

I responded with all the sincerity and youthful optimism I could muster: "Jack, you're right. But, you know, tough times call for determined and visionary leadership. You have given that combination to the Jack Eckerd Corporation. If you will help me, I will try to do the same for the college. I am a Marine veteran and about as patriotic as you can get. And let's not read too much into the behavior of students. They are young and will adjust to the changing times as they get older. We were all young once. The main point is that they are bright and will be running things tomorrow."

"True," he replied, "but what about the faculty?"

"Faculty, too," I answered as softly and engagingly as I could, "are reflections of the times. I know the faculty very well and consider myself one of them. They are among America's finest."

"Well," he began, "I never graduated from college, but I believe in Florida's future and having a strong private sector in higher education is important. I also like the idea that we are building something new, ambitious, and promising. And what is life without a challenge? Risk is critical to progress." In Eckerd's words I could hear echoes of Adolph Rupp—the same positive, confident, can-do tone; the excitement in doing something new; the attraction to risk; the belief in progress.

"But," he concluded, "no promises. Let's see what happens."

Over the next three three years, the college borrowed some $1.5 million for current operations to continue to build a national reputation and attract a major donor. We gambled that eventually we would name the college for a major donor in the Duke, Harvard, Stanford, Vanderbilt tradition. Meanwhile, Jack Eckerd continued to be involved as a trustee and as an advisor to me. He had attended board meetings regularly and we had become good friends through my writings on education theory and practice, his belief that I was struggling mightily, and because I helped him with speech writing and positions on public issues as he became involved in politics.

I drove to his Clearwater office again in early 1971. We greeted warmly and I moved immediately to the issue. "Jack, as a trustee, you know the situation at the college well." I paused, swallowed deeply, braced my back, and with all the executive and persuasive rhetoric I could muster, continued, "I have given the college my best shot. We have a splendid academic program with bright students and outstanding faculty. But that huge debt from the early years is killing us. We need help and need it fast."

Then my punch line: "As we have talked before, some day the lights will go out on Eckerd Drugs. You will likely merge or be absorbed by a larger company. And the day is coming when you will not be running the company. If you really want to leave a legacy, you will put your name on this college and thus ensure your values in perpetuity. Colleges change their names only once." I paused, catching my breath, wanting to finish before getting his response. "The college is high quality, private, innovative, and has great potential. All the things you stand for. Are there any circumstances under which you would give the college $10 million? If you would do that, it would be an honor for me to recommend that the college become Eckerd College. I know you don't want that, but to be in the company of John Harvard, Leland Stanford, James B. Duke, and Cornelius Vanderbilt will be a source of joy and pride for your friends and family."

I stopped, waiting for his response. It came in a surprising question: "Will $10 million do it?"

"We will need a lot more, but this would pay off the short-term debt and give us a base endowment from which to build," I responded.

His next response was less encouraging. "I probably won't do it, but it is an interesting idea."

"Could I," I asked, "submit a proposal outlining the powerful development this would be for America, Florida, and higher education?"

"Sure," he responded, "but I don't think I'm interested."

And so, on a sunny Sunday afternoon, in mid-February 1971, following church, I took a yellow pad and pencil to the atrium of Lewis House, the president's residence at Florida Presbyterian. The morning sermon had been on the Biblical verse, "Where there is no vision, the people perish."

I penned a handwritten, seventeen-page document outlining the rationale for "Jack Eckerd College." On Monday, I delivered the proposal to Clearwater. Two and one-half torturous months passed, and I was getting discouraged. But I knew Jack well enough to know that he would tell me when he was ready.

The call came during a visit to my family's summer home in Blowing Rock, North Carolina, in mid-May. "Dr. Wireman," Eckerd's assistant informed me, "Mr. Eckerd wants to talk with you." I could hardly contain my anticipation and excitement.

"Billy, sometime when you have a minute, come by," he stated softly. "I have reviewed your proposal. I still probably won't do it, but let's get together." We closed with a few pleasantries, and I immediately notified my son, Gary, to pack up because we were returning promptly to St. Petersburg.

Two days later I visited with Jack Eckerd, and he agreed to make a $10 million gift to Florida Presbyterian College. It was, at that time, the largest gift by an individual to a college or university in Florida's history. The name change was not a condition of the gift for him. A week later, he brought me a small, personal, handwritten check to retire the $1.5 million operating debt with instructions to get to the bank before 2 P.M. so we wouldn't have to pay that day's interest on the loans.

In June 1971, three years after my first meeting with Eckerd, I joyfully announced his $10 million gift. On my recommendation, Florida Presbyterian officially became Eckerd College on July 1, 1972. On that occasion, Jack Eckerd told *Fortune*, "This is the best investment I ever made."

In 1987, Charles Paul Conn wrote:

> Jack Eckerd may be the youngest seventy-three-year-old man in the country. He is a legendary figure in the business world, a senior statesman in the Florida political community . . . a full-dimensioned citizen . . . a barnstorming pilot . . . he helped pioneer an aggressive brand of marketing that put the word "entrepreneur" into the American vocabulary (*Eckerd*, p. 11-12).

That Jack Eckerd was one of my teachers.
What Adolph Rupp did for basketball, Eckerd did for

retail. He practically invented the modern American drugstore chain. He was a success, I think, in large part because he was virtually born in a drugstore. His dad had started in the drugstore business in 1898, and by the time Jack was born in 1913 his dad had put together a small chain of a dozen stores. As a young man, Jack worked in the basements of his dad's stores, opening boxes, sorting merchandise; upstairs, he waited on customers and counted the day's income.

In his youth, Jack managed two of his dad's stores, and immersed himself in the details of the business, and years later, as the CEO of Jack Eckerd Corporation, Jack still loved to get involved in the details of his stores (*Eckerd*, p. 197).

From the first, Jack loved the game of business. It wasn't really about money. Money was great and Jack Eckerd is rightly proud of the wealth he produced. But, money was not an end so much as a means, a means of keeping score. "I love to compete," Jack always said. (*Eckerd*, p. 181)

Like Rupp, Eckerd was very, very good at his game. In his autobiography, he wrote:

> Assessing my business career, I can see that I was working for the Game. That was the source of my fulfillment— winning at the Game. And it was a great Game, that of beating the competition in an honest fight where the public renders the decision of who has won and lost. . . . Winning at the Game was one of the delights of my life . . . I loved the Game, and I think the record shows I played it well (*Eckerd*, p. 175).

One of Jack's great passions was to stay close to the

business, to listen to the employees on the floor. His people were his business, he often said. In 1970, Jack ran for Florida governor and was defeated by Rubin Askew; later, after a friendly visit with Governor Askew in Tallahassee, Jack and I drove to one of his stores in Valdosta, Georgia. You can imagine the shock tremors of the Eckerd employees, especially the management, when the word spread that "the old man" was on the floor. But those who knew their business had no reason for alarm. His questions were penetrating but soft: What were people buying? What were the major complaints? What is asked for most often that we don't have? Is this a happy shop? How can we do it better? Is our central office helpful to you, the people who make the company go?

Jack was a little boy when Charles Lindbergh was America's daring hero, and young Jack Eckerd wanted to be just like him. In his early twenties, Jack buzzed around the skies of Erie, Pennsylvania, dreaming of becoming another Lucky Lindy. But after several airplane crashes, Jack decided that maybe going into the family business was the direction to take after all. He told his dad, who replied,

> I don't care if you go into this business or not. But if you do, you're going to work harder than anyone else around here. I'll tell you that! If your name is Eckerd, that means you come earlier and stay later. You've got a job if you want it, but I'm not going to have you messing up my business just because you're my son (*Eckerd*, p. 17)!

Jack worked hard. In fact, he came to see hard work as one of the great values in life. He found himself, I think, by losing himself in the work before him.

Eckerd was a worker, but he was also a master builder. His story is one of the great stories in American business. He took two rickety drugstores that he bought with money he borrowed from his brother, and built a multi-million dollar business empire. By 1972, Eckerd Drugs had 342 stores across America serviced by seven thousand employees. And that wasn't all. Eckerd Drugs by then included a small chain of department stores and two other companies, Gray Security Services and the Kurman Company, a food service firm. The Eckerd Corporation continued to prosper. By the time Eckerd eventually sold the business in 1986, through expansion and various mergers and acquisitions, the company operated some 1,700 retail stores,

No, Jack didn't build that organization single-handedly. But he was its driving force. However, Jack didn't simply create a money-making machine. He built a powerful, effective, and efficient organization. More than that, he helped enliven and invigorate the entire American marketplace.

Jack insisted that America's economic architecture needed rebuilding. A book he wrote with Chuck Colson offers little if any technical, or legal, or even commercial advice. Instead, their blueprint for the reconstruction of American commerce is fundamentally a design for moral reconstruction. They call Americans to adopt these six principles:

1. **The Value of the Worker**. As Martin Luther said, every job is to glorify God, and every worker is infinitely

valuable. All who labor . . . must be treated with respect and dignity.

2. **Walking and Talking in the Trenches**. Ivory-tower management doesn't work; managers need to lead their forces by going to the front lines themselves.

3. **Responsibility and the Pursuit of Excellence**. No work that is less than our best can be personally meaningful or rewarding.

4. **The Value of Training**. Developing the skills of employees is not only good for the individual . . . it also makes them more valuable to the organization.

5. **Dollars and Sense**. This is the profit motive . . . for most [people] the greatest motivation comes from incentive pay and healthy competition.

6. **Working to Serve**. Effective leadership includes enabling others to meet goals. No one said it better than Jesus: He, who would lead, let him serve (*America*, 130).

Paradoxically, Jack Eckerd's commitment of $10 million to the school that now bears his name proved that he was a man both deeply rooted in his past and restlessly drawn to the future. He believed deeply in American traditions of civility and respect for law, but he also knew that the future belonged to the young. His capacity to blend these two qualities pinpoints a critical factor in human progress: The ability to look beyond the rawness and volatility of the moment and see the big picture.

On the one hand, Eckerd hated rehashing the past. His wife, Ruth, joked that after she and Jack played tennis, she would often comment on what she could have done and should have done, which always irritated him. He once told a TV interviewer: "The only way I can stay sane is to never look back" (*Eckerd*, p. 12). Whenever someone attempted to begin Monday-morning-quarterbacking, Jack's inevitable, exasperated comment would be "let's just move ahead."

Yet, Jack respected tradition. The past was not a prison for him, but a rich, nurturing soil that gave him confidence and direction. Business was an Eckerd family tradition. By the time Jack sold Eckerd Drugs to a consortium of investors in 1986, he and his parents and his family had put more than a century of their lives into the business.

As rooted as Jack was in the past, he was tugged relentlessly by the future. From the very beginning of his life in the family business, Jack was an experimenter and risk-taker. His dad thought of drugstores as Victorian apothecaries—dark, sober shops with mysterious flasks stacked high up on the walls, serviced by eccentric clerks. Jack, as early as the late 1940s, thought of drugstores as active, lively, aggressive, all-purpose stores—as a cross between department stores and old-time general stores.

Jack's daddy sold only drugs and medical supplies; Jack sold just about everything. In his dad's stores, merchandise was hidden, and there was no shopping; in Jack's stores, merchandise was out on display, and everything possible was done to encourage shopping. Jack's dad experimented with pricing; Jack experimented with everything—prices, advertising, floor layout, location, and special promotions. Jack's dad cautiously sewed together a dozen stores in several different cities in Pennsylvania and New York; Jack constructed a vast retail chain which stretched across America.

Eckerd's capacity to keep the best of the old, but add new ideas was very evident in his relationship with, for instance, George Jenkins, owner of Publix Supermarkets, a giant Florida supermarket chain. Jenkins, headquartered in Lakeland, called Eckerd with some interesting research findings: In shopping centers, if a drugstore was located close to a supermarket, both enterprises did significantly better in sales than if they stood alone. Would Eckerd, Jenkins inquired, be interested in teaming with him to place an Eckerd drugstore next to a Publix supermarket as he expanded throughout Florida? Eckerd jumped at the chance of a lifetime, and this proximity to Publix, coupled with his new concept of a retail drugstore offering a variety of products, which could be selected from aisles, became the formula for Eckerd's success. He kept the best of the old—clean stores, courteous service, fair prices, but added two new twists: a more comprehensive shopping menu and proximity to Publix. There were no gimmicks here, no slick claims—just solid innovation tied to values of the shopper. A combination pharmacy and retail shop offering a wide variety of clothing, cosmetics, food, and other personal items had replaced the traditional drugstore. Customers loved the new idea and flocked to it by the thousands. Jack Eckerd had blended the old and the new into a winning combination.

He was astonishingly successful. Why? He later wrote:

> The point is not that I had more drugstore savvy than my father—far from it . . . The point is that the drugstore business was changing, fundamental shifts were occurring in the buying habits of the whole country, and as a result the

rules of the game were being rewritten (*Eckerd*, p. 41).

Charles Paul Conn, who helped Jack write his memoirs, describes Jack as a "pilot/tycoon/candidate/philanthropist/ corporate executive/public servant" (*Eckerd*, p. 13). He was all that and more. It wasn't simply that he had an amazingly open mind and vigorous curiosity; rather, it's that he had trained himself, like some frontier scout, to feel the ground, taste the wind, sniff the air, hear the slightest snap of the twigs, and see the faintest rustle in the bush. After a while, Jack, like Daniel Boone, could do this instinctively and intuitively.

When he returned from military service in World War II, and entered the family business, Jack knew that something fundamental had changed in America's commercial forest. No economist or sociologist, Jack still knew that more and more people would have more and more money to spend; that a retail business that served a mass audience would grow quickly; that what consumers wanted was speed and convenience and variety; that providing the greatest possible service at the lowest possible price would be the formula for retail success; that rapid organizational growth was not only possible but essential in the 1950s and 1960s. Jack, you see, had an uncanny ability to connect things, to connect his personal experience with that of others, his little world with the wider world around him, his business sense with the needs of his customers. He later wrote:

As I settled back into the routine of the drugstore business in Wilmington and Erie, in the late 1940s, I was vaguely aware that a fundamental shift was occurring in the way people shopped for the goods we were selling. Like many other businessmen of that time, it was not a thing that I understood intellectually, so much as it was something I sensed. It was less a matter of analysis and more a matter of intuition that told me things were changing. I began to sniff the air (*Eckerd*, p. 45).

Timing is everything, and timing depends on being able to connect, being able to catch the gestalt. Jack writes:

> In the building of a big business, a critical element always is timing, that right combination of events and conditions, most of which are beyond the control of the players themselves. Some people call it fate; some say it's in the stars; I have come to understand it as the hand of the Lord. But however one explains it, timing is everything (*Eckerd*, p. 41).

Eckerd always had a sense of social responsibility about his wealth. He was especially interested in troubled youth that normal agencies could not handle. His Wilderness Camp idea was revolutionary at the time: Youngsters would work in teams, and the key to any move was to achieve agreement by all team members on the project. As you can imagine, this proved to be extraordinarily difficult. I visited these camps several times and often watched as twelve- and thirteen-year-olds would be immobilized from a lack of agreement by a recalcitrant member. But the principle was inviolate: All had to agree. This process engaged some of the most fundamental skills of living: patience, understanding other points of view, capacity to express one's views when you disagree, forgiveness, and many others. Jack saw this process as important to success in life. Thus this connection could help youngsters develop into responsible citizens. His rationale: Those are our kids. If we don't help them, they will continue to be troublemakers, and we will be denied their talents in building a strong society.

Jack Eckerd was a businessman who was also a passionate patriot.

Like others of the "greatest generation," Jack, in 1941, after Pearl Harbor, rushed to enlist. He spent the four years of the war as a military pilot. For part of that time, he flew over Burma's dangerous mountains, "flew the hump," as the veterans say.

During the 1950s and 1960s, Jack built his company. But the need to participate in the wider community, the need to be a citizen, never left him.

In the 1960s, Jack became involved in politics. Why? Lots of reasons, no doubt. He loved to compete. He had made all the money he'd ever need. He had become one of the top players in his business, and there was nowhere higher to go. Like many of his generation, he thought of public service as an honorable enterprise. And, he said later, he felt that he owed it to his community to somehow give something back. "I began to ask myself what I had ever done as a way of repaying this debt" (*Eckerd*, 114).

His later involvement in public life was earlier implied in his basic business principles. When asked how he constructed such an enormous and successful enterprise, Jack relayed:

My experience with Eckerd Drugs taught me that the company that has the best chance of rapid, solid growth is the company that:

1. Understands that its best asset is its employees.

2. Dares to do something different from what everyone else is doing.

3. Makes decisions on the basis of fairness to the public, the employees, and the stockholders (*Eckerd*, p. 102).

No one doubted Jack's daring. He liked to say, "Anything worthwhile requires the risk of losing, and that is a risk I have always been willing to take" (*Eckerd*, p. 133). What people didn't always understand were his first and third points, his deep social dedication to his employees and to the public at large. Given this dedication, it's no wonder that Jack got involved in politics.

Oddly enough, the first public service job was probably the worst job he ever had.

In 1970, Jack, a conservative Republican, ran for Florida governor and was defeated; he then ran for the U.S. Senate, and was defeated again. No, not everyone voted for Jack, but just about everyone came to admire his remarkable entrepreneurial skills and his blunt honesty. In 1974, President Gerald Ford asked him to take on the utterly thankless task of administering the General Services Administration (GSA). The GSA is the federal government's supply agency. In Jack's day, GSA had around 35,000 employees; it managed some one hundred million square feet of office space; and in twenty-one regional warehouses, it stocked everything from paper clips to helicopters. It was, Jack remembered, "a bureaucratic quagmire" (*Eckerd*, 138). Who better to manage it than the king of retail?

It was a thankless task, but a vital one. Why did Jack accept it? Not for the pay, certainly not for the glory! No, I think he accepted the job because it needed doing, because it was a challenge, but above all, because he felt a profound and patriotic need to give back to the wider community.

I remember, a few years earlier, in the spring of 1971, a group of college trustees urged me to apply to join the Lakewood Country Club, south St. Petersburg's most prestigious and elitist club. I am not a golfer, but it would have been nice to be able to use the dining and tennis facilities at the club. Additionally, as president of Eckerd College, I would be in contact with the city's "movers and shakers," never a bad thing for fund raising.

Well, the club refused my admission. I was told that several members of the admissions committee saw my membership as a prelude to my bringing my black friends to the club, which at the time did not have any black members. I was upset but not surprised. Eckerd College in general, and the faculty and students in particular, were seen as very liberal; some in St. Petersburg would even say radical. I was, of course, associated with that perception, even though I had a lot of personal friends in the club. Jack Eckerd was outraged by what happened and called me with a personal apology. He was not a member but did write the committee extolling my virtues and pointing out what an injustice this was. He also wrote a letter to the editor of the *St. Petersburg Times* saying how very stupid and unfair this was. I was encouraged to reapply, but I did not. Jack and I often talked about this incident.

Jack thought of himself as a "conservative." He told me, though, several times that where he differed with some of his conservative friends was over the issue of equal opportunity. A person should be judged on merit and talent and not color or religion. This was America; that's how Americans did things. Racial or religious bigotry was just plain wrong.

Thanks to Jack Eckerd, our little college, Eckerd College, prospered. It had all been very hard work, and by the fall of 1976, I was tired. For sixteen years I had poured myself into building the college. The average tenure of college presidents was four years—I was coming upon nine years in what one reporter called "the toughest and best job in America." Jack's immense gift had saved the college, but every day is a fight for financial survival for young, ambitious private colleges. I was weary. Several close friends urged me to speak with Jack.

On the Wednesday morning before Thanksgiving 1976, I called him in Washington where he was wrestling with the GSA and told him I needed to talk. Jack urged me to catch a flight to D.C.; he would have a car meet me at the airport.

When we met, he sensed something was up and quickly asked, "What's on your mind, Billy?"

I got right to the point. "Is it time for me to step aside and give the college fresh leadership?" I still loved the little place but wondered if I was the person to continue the struggle. There are times when even the "man in the arena" is simply bone-tired.

Jack listened, and then said, "Billy, I can't tell you what to do. You saved the college, and your legacy there is secure. But you have to do what you think is best for you and your family. You are still young, and you have a career or two ahead of you. I experienced the same thing with my company. You just get tired."

He asked if a sabbatical would help, but I said no, I thought I badly needed a change. He asked if I wanted to go into business. I said no, recalling my parting conversation with Adolph Rupp about feeling called to an academic life. Like Jack, I thought about politics. Then there were our family responsibilities in Daytona Beach—a beach lodge, restaurant, and fishing pier. I simply didn't know which way to turn.

Jack gave me excellent advice: "Billy, you're tired. Don't do anything rash or hasty. Get your bearings. And stay in educational leadership. You have a lot to offer."

He sensed my struggle and told me to think about it and let him know. He then asked if I would like to tour Washington with him. I agreed of course. For the next two hours, we drove around in his government car. His driver was a history buff and showed us sights I had never seen. Jack and I chatted along the way, never mentioning the earlier conversation; yet, it was clear that this self-styled "hardheaded businessman" sensed my pain and wanted to help.

Later, he dropped me off at the airport, went in to ensure that my plane was on time and then, as we parted, shook my hand firmly and said, "Whatever happens, Billy, you and I have done a good thing. Let's not forget that. I gave that money as much to you as to the college."

I felt much better after our meeting. Jack Eckerd had been where I was. He had felt frustration and conflict between his devotion to his company and his gnawing feeling that he perhaps should move on.

I left Eckerd College the following spring. Jack was always in my corner, and we stayed in touch as friends. He asked me what he could do to help the transition to my successor. I suggested that he assume the interim presidency at Eckerd. That would be a tremendous show of confidence to the world that he was still behind the college. He did. And that's how Jack Eckerd, the king of retail, briefly became a college president.

As for me, I moved on. In the spring of 1978, following a brief stint as a dean at Rollins College, I became president of Queens College in Charlotte, North Carolina. After assuming the presidency, I got a call from Jack's assistant. Jack, I was told, planned to visit Jim Bakker's "Praise the Lord" (PTL) program in South Carolina. Could he see me while in Charlotte? Of course, I replied, but I could do better than that: I would arrange a luncheon in his honor at the Charlotte City Club. After lunch, I asked Jack if he would like to speak briefly to the group of a dozen or so. He explained his mission of going to PTL and said that his deepening Christian faith called him to witness for the Lord. A guest asked if he felt uneasy about appearing on a controversial program like PTL. No, he replied, PTL has a huge following and if he could influence one person through his appearance, the trip would be worthwhile. He emphasized that his appearance did not translate into endorsement of PTL, but that "anytime you have an audience willing to listen to the Lord's word, you should take advantage of it."

Here was yet another side to Jack Eckerd, to him, the most important side.

Jack Eckerd died in 2004 at age ninety-one. He was already well up in years when the *Tampa Tribune* wrote of him:

Eckerd epitomizes the storybook image of a benevolent

American capitalist . . . [He] has donated his time, energy, and millions of dollars to causes that reach far beyond the checkout counters of the drugstore chain. It was not enough for Eckerd simply to make money. He put it to work raising a kingdom full of larger-than-life accomplishments (*Eckerd*, p. 12).

Jack was a business tycoon. A candidate for governor and senator. A top federal official. He was a citizen and patriot. He was also a teacher.

In fact, Jack was convinced that teaching was a leader's most important task. A great leader, in Jack's book, was not someone who scrambled to fortune and fame on others' backs. No, a great leader was someone who helped others cultivate their abilities, who helped others grow and prosper and flourish.

As he built his business, Jack constantly stressed the importance of his co-workers. The organization's success was directly linked, he was absolutely sure, to their success.

By the late 1960s, as a prosperous and famous entrepreneur, Jack became even more engaged in teaching. Using the wealth he'd generated, he and Ruth founded Eckerd Youth Alternatives, Inc., in 1968. Eckerd Youth Alternatives was a program which tried to help emotionally troubled kids get straight by engaging them in intensive counseling and challenging outdoor experience. Jack also became an even more crucial supporter of Florida Presbyterian College. Jack and Ruth were major supporters of the Clearwater Performing Arts Center and Theater. They created the Eckerd Foundation, a unique private enterprise that coordinates the work of Florida's juvenile detention center in Okeechobee. Jack and Ruth also organized Florida's Prison Rehabilitative Industries and Diversified Enterprises, Inc. (PRIDE), a private business that operates Florida's prison industries.

He was also a man of intense faith.

Raised a Christian, Jack described himself for most of his life as a "casual Christian." Certainly not an evil man, he was not exactly a spiritual man either. At the very height of his commercial success, in the late 1960s, he was a deeply dissatisfied man.

He explains in his own words:

"Though I did not understand it at the time, the restlessness I felt in 1969 was one of the first symptoms of a serious problem: I had a peculiar kind of hunger inside me that all my success in business had not satisfied. There was something missing in my life, and I was beginning to sense it, vaguely at first, then more and more strongly" (*Eckerd*, p. 114).

Looking back he would write: "What I was feeling was a spiritual restlessness" (*Eckerd*, p. 156).

Jack never "got religion" in any stereotypical way. There was no sudden emotional explosion, no drastic turn from wickedness to goodness. Instead, when he was already in his sixties, when he was one of America's most influential businessmen, Jack's faith began to grow, to deepen. He saw a neighbor overcome alcoholism, and began joining him in morning Bible study. As he got involved with Florida's prisons, he met former NFL player and Christian leader, Bill Glass. Later still, he worked closely with Chuck Colson and Colson's prison ministry.

What he discovered, in the late 1970s and early 1980s, was

a whole dimension of his life that had been missing, or rather, a dimension that had been stirring and growing for years unknown to him. What happened? He would write later: "For those people who want me to tell them when and how I was born again, my answer is, 'I don't know—it didn't happen overnight'" (*Eckerd*, 163).

He began to pray regularly. He began to read the Scriptures in a new, powerful, personal way. He began to think of God not simply as a kind of "reality out there," but as "God for me." It was as if something inside of him that had been blurred for years came into sharp focus. It was gradual, to be sure, but profound. Chuck Colson would say of Eckerd, "He is a totally different person" (*Eckerd*, p. 170).

What had Jack found?

"I have a peace of mind I never had in seventy years; I have a confidence that I can seek personal guidance from God, in the Bible, and in prayer" (*Eckerd*, p. 164).

Jack had found coherence and direction; inner peace and outer purpose. It wasn't so much that a "new Jack" had suddenly emerged as that the "real Jack," so long only a potential, had suddenly become apparent.

Jack wrote that this surprising burst of spiritual growth was hard in some ways.

"For many successful men and women, it is our egos that God has trouble getting us to submit to Him . . . there is another reason we hesitate to ascribe our business and professional success to the hand of God: to do so requires us to place all that we own at His disposal. If He gave it to us, then we must be willing to give it back to Him and His kingdom, rather than hoarding it for ourselves" (*Eckerd*, p. 173).

Yet this spiritual growth brought Jack riches he had never imagined. He learned the difference between stewardship and ownership; the importance of giving not getting; the centrality of the Kingdom, not his career. He learned to say "not my will but Thine," and mean it. And all this brought immense joy. "No amount of success and no amount of civic duty has ever given me the personal fulfillment that I have found by submitting my life to Jesus Christ," Jack would write (*Eckerd*, p. 174).

Jack had the restless energy and ferocious hunger for competition that drives people like Adolph Rupp. Yet from the very beginning, people who knew Jack knew that there was a kind of bedrock ethical imperative beneath all this struggle and competition, a bedrock that became more and more prominent over time.

Yes, Jack was a fearsome competitor, but there were some things he would not do, some actions he would not take because, along with his competitive instincts, he had a powerful sense of honor.

It appeared in details. His longtime friend and colleague Rex Farrior recalls, for instance, that once Jack got interested in opening a chain of liquor stores. He was the king of retail, after all. His thousand drugstores were humming. Why not branch out into other sorts of retail operations?

There was just one problem. In many states, state governments controlled liquor sales. You had to get a license to sell liquor. And in some of these states, you had to pay a little something under the table to state officials to get the license you needed.

It would be a lucrative business. There was no doubt that the Eckerd team could quickly dominate retail liquor sales. All it would take were a few bribes here and there, and everything would be arranged. How did Jack respond? When he heard about it he said: "Forget it. Just forget it. If I can't do business on top of the table, I don't do business at all!" (*Eckerd*, p. 110).

Rex Farrior once remarked: "When a man has money, if you want to judge him, find out two things: how he made it and what he does with it" (*Eckerd*, p. 111). Jack's way told him to make his money honestly, and then give it away generously. When he was up in years, Jack came to respect a company called Servicemaster. It was a nuts-and-bolts sort of company, nothing fancy. Servicemaster provided, among other things, beds to hospitals. What Jack admired about it was its ethic, the company's four guiding principles, listed in order of priority. They were:

1. to honor God in all we do.
2. to help people develop.
3. to pursue excellence.
4. to grow profitably (*Eckerd*, p. 185).

This might well have been Jack Eckerd's personal motto as a servant leader. It is how he lived his life; it is how he taught me to live my life, too.

Bill Lee

3

BILL LEE:
THE EVER-CHEERFUL OPTIMIST

"He lived life to the fullest—whether it was building his company, the community, or the state's economy. He lived with a passion for the things he believed in."

—JIM HUNT
FORMER N.C. GOVERNOR

Not light them for themselves; Heaven does with us as we with torches do, for if our virtues Do not go forth of us, 'twere all alike. As if we had them not.

—SHAKESPEARE
Measure for Measure

It was a hot summer day in late August 1987 as Queens College prepared for a momentous occasion. A sparkling sun bathed the oak-studded campus with a warm glow as guests arrived. A sense of excitement and anticipation filled the air.

The setting: Burwell Parlors in Burwell Hall, the main administration building of the Queens campus.

The occasion: A press conference to announce that after a

yearlong study, Queens was embarking on a bold new course to "position the college for the twenty-first century." The press turned out in full force, and the room buzzed with curious television and newspaper reporters. Also in attendance were Queens trustees, faculty, students, staff, alumnae, and friends who wanted to be present at this historic moment in the life of an institution they loved. The format of the press conference called for Bill Lee, Queens's board chairman, to announce the biggest and most important decision: Queens, after 130 years as a women's college, was going coed.

The decision to go coed was more than simply an admissions decision. It affected the whole identity, the whole culture, of the college. Students, alums, faculty, trustees, and staff were deeply committed to Queens, and such a change was emotionally charged. A blue-ribbon committee composed of representatives from Queens's internal and external communities had pondered the question of Queens's future and arrived at a general consensus on which direction Queens should go. It was the best thing to do, but it was risky. Now it was time to get on with it.

Chairman Bill Lee opened the news conference with a powerful and upbeat statement about the importance of Queens to Charlotte and how going coed, along with the other bold initiatives we planned, would take Queens to new heights of distinction and service. He then called on me for the details of our plan. I opened with a strong endorsement of Lee's view on the wisdom of our new course. Then I launched into a point-by-point summary of the new initiatives: In addition to going coed, we planned to expand the size of the faculty, increase faculty and staff salaries by 50 percent in five years, and recommit to being a major player in serving Charlotte's burgeoning adult learners, especially in business education. Plus, we would launch two hugely ambitious new projects—an international experience program that would guarantee all undergraduates an opportunity to travel abroad, and an internship program for all students, which would make sure that every student had the chance to engage in meaningful work in the world beyond the academy. And, oh yes, we also planned to revise radically our core liberal arts program.

That August 1987 day was for me one of those breathtaking moments when you tack the ship, feel it play off well, watch the sails billow, and know that you're headed on a grand adventure. We knew that what we were doing was good. Later, our plan would be described by Johnetta Cole, the distinguished then-president of Atlanta's Spelman College, "as the most unique and relevant undergraduate experience in America."

So there I was, speaking to a crowd of reporters, my remarks flashed out around the region by the television cameras. I was nervous, and when I'm nervous, I get very serious. Especially when half a dozen television cameras are staring at me.

About four minutes into my presentation, Bill Lee got up from his seat and walked to the back of the room. Then, he held up a huge card with the advice: "Smile, Billy. Be cheerful! It's a great day." I got the message, relaxed from what he later described as my "chin first, stern Marine bearing," and finished my presentation.

Bill Lee's message captures for me the essence of that great man: Smile; be cheerful; be optimistic; it's a great day.

Perhaps you didn't know Bill Lee. Let me tell you about him.

How had I gotten before all those reporters and cameras? How had I gotten to Queens in the first place? It was all Bill Lee's doing.

When he asked me eight years before to come to Queens, I was reluctant at first, but the more I learned about Charlotte and Queens, I saw it was an offer I could not refuse. The Chinese have a word that, depending on its pronunciation, means either challenge or opportunity. I was in the market for both. Queens was looking for a president who could help it through a rough patch of spiraling costs and low admissions and restore the institution's luster. After my years at Eckerd College, I knew what I could do in education, and I was eager to continue my own development in a new arena. I had worked with Adolph Rupp, a master motivator and molder of champions. I had worked with Jack Eckerd, an entrepreneur and successful innovator in the retail business. Now I was to learn from captains of industry and banking. It was the kind of challenge I thrive on, and the opportunity to work in a dynamic city with dynamic civic leaders greatly appealed to me.

Bill Lee was chairman and CEO of Duke Power Company, one of the nation's leading public utilities. Within a year after he spoke with me, he would be dealing with the aftermath of the Three Mile Island radiation leak and serving as chair of the Institute of Nuclear Power Operators, which he helped form. And yet he could give his prestige, time, and boundless energy to a small liberal arts college nestled in the cozy neighborhood of Myers Park, close to his home in Charlotte. I would work closely with Lee during his tenure as chairman of the Queens board of trustees from 1985 to 1991; in those years, I learned to respect and admire him. He became, for me, one of the incarnations of what much later I'd understand as servant leadership.

Bill Lee was one of America's power wizards. A cross between an entrepreneur and engineer, Lee ran one of the largest power grids in the nation. Like my other teachers, he was first of all a master of his craft. He not only ran Duke Power, he also helped create and chair the World Association of Nuclear Power Operators in the wake of the Chernobyl nuclear disaster in 1987, was named the utility sector "CEO of the Decade" by *Financial World* magazine, and was the recognized expert and ambassador for nuclear energy worldwide.

Like Jack Eckerd, Bill Lee was a kind of master builder. He loved action, projects, and challenges. He loved to get things started, nurse things along, build things up, and create things that hadn't existed before. Like Theodore Roosevelt's "man in the arena," Bill Lee loved the sweat and dirt and grime of honest labor.

He became my friend.

Once, when I asked him why in the world he had assumed the chairmanship of the board of trustees of Queens when he had so many other exhausting responsibilities, he said: "I have to go where I am most needed. Queens is an institution of my church, and it's in the neighborhood. Additionally, it is important for Charlotte to have Queens succeed. I want to do my part in making that happen."

I never put much stock in phrenology until I met Bill Lee. If ever there was a man whose exterior demeanor and physical appearance accurately reflected his innermost being, it was William States Lee. His full cheeks and ruddy complexion with eyes sparkling beneath those trademark bushy eyebrows signaled his warmth and enthusiasm for all things human. His heart, which he gave so willingly to all who needed his particular gifts, shone brightly in those eyes and in that face. His impish grin flashed like a traffic signal, warning that a joke was on the way or that a keen insight had just made a synaptic connection in his energetic brain.

Lee, in appearance and personality, was a sanguine man. A cheerful man. A natural-born optimist. His optimism was boundless, his enthusiasm unfettered, and his vision for the future was clear. This, I was to learn as I worked and planned and imagined with him, was what drew people to him, what made him the accomplished leader he was. "It was the sheer force of his personality that attracted you," says Ed Crutchfield, former chairman and CEO of First Union Bank. "Some people will have influence because of their position, but I don't think there was anybody more able to call the troops together and move an issue than Bill Lee."

I hadn't known Bill Lee before I moved to Charlotte, but when I met him I sensed some of those leadership abilities I had seen before. At home anywhere in the world, restless with plans and projects and sheer raw energy, an enthusiastic traveler, fundamentally dissatisfied with any status quo, Bill Lee was also deeply and firmly rooted in his city and state and church. Always on the move, there was something rock solid and utterly immovable about him. I had seen that odd combination of rootedness and restlessness before, and I knew that it signaled something very powerful in a person. And then there was that same vision that I had known in Rupp and Eckerd, that uncanny ability both to see how disparate parts go together, and to see the future already alive in the present.

A person cannot really be summarized in a single word. But, sometimes there is such an omnipresent trait in a person that a single word or phrase just might target that person's greatness or his claim on our memory. For Hamlet, it was his melancholy. Abraham Lincoln was "Honest Abe." And Ronald Reagan was "the great communicator." In Bill Lee's case, the phase is "energy and optimism." Bill Lee had an unbridled energy that sparked from his eyes and put the curl in those bushy eyebrows. He was restless in his drive to identify needs, find solutions, and do good wherever he could. His pulse, I believe, was measured in kilowatts.

And it was with energy and optimism that Lee made his great contributions to North Carolina, the nation and the world. He was born in 1929, the newest member of a prominent Charlotte family, and grandson of W. S. Lee, Sr., a civil engineer who along with J. D. and Ben Duke and W. Gill Wylie formed Southern Power Company, the forerunner of Duke Power. Around the turn of the century, they began building hydroelectric stations along the Catawba River, a move that helped energize the southern Piedmont and rural North Carolina. Electricity, it seems, was in Bill Lee's blood.

By most accounts, Lee's early childhood was charmed. He attended prep school at Virginia's prestigious Woodberry Forest, then college at Princeton where he earned a degree in engineering that featured a physics class with Robert Oppenheimer, one of the greatest physicists of the twentieth century and one of the architects of the atomic bomb. Lee graduated *magna cum laude* and Phi Beta Kappa in 1951. From his mother Sarah Toy, Lee inherited a wide-ranging curiosity and love of learning, which he indulged at Princeton by taking a poetry course with T. S. Eliot. Throughout his life this eclectic intellectual curiosity displayed itself in interests from Egyptology and classical music to jazz, woodworking, and gardening. Lee's devotion to and support of higher education, including the "little college up the street," can be traced, I imagine, to the early influence of his artistic mother and the first-rate education he received.

His determination and drive are likewise derived from these early years. It is not well-known, but in the early forties, just as young Bill was coming of age, his family experienced hard times when his father left the family. Lee's daughter Lisa Lee Morgan relates that although born to wealth, her father had to watch his mother auction off silver, move into a smaller house, and go to work in a torpedo factory. Bill Lee, she observed, saw the limits of wealth. He learned to place more value on strength of character than on material possessions. He inherited nothing but his parents' brilliance.

Maybe it was that humbling experience that taught young Bill Lee something he would never forget. Maybe it was his deep religious faith that rooted in him a sense that whatever we have, we receive as gifts and care for as stewards. Anyway, early on it dawned on him that his electric personality, his optimism, and his intellect were gifts, not things he had earned, not things he owned, and I think it was then that his core personality took shape, a personality marked by gratitude and joy.

And somehow then, convinced that he himself had been

given so many gifts, he became convinced that he had a duty to give to others. He would do well in business and recover much of his family's lost wealth, but what impressed others later was not Bill Lee's power or money but his unflagging commitment to his city and country. Civic involvement was simply second nature to him. I would learn quickly that when asked, as he was countless times, to serve on a board or lend his name to a cause, Bill Lee never sent an associate or provided only his name. He went himself and he lent his time and expertise. And he did it in all humility. Whenever I asked him for something or called him to do something for Queens he would say, "I'd be honored to do it." The CEO of Duke Power, the world-renowned entrepreneur and power engineer, *Financial World*'s "CEO of the Decade" would be honored to take on yet another task for Queens!

One particular incident stands out: I was with a group that called on Lee for a gift to a major Queens fund-raising campaign. The ask was made, and he responded: "I will do that and more. Give me five prominent prospects, and I will call on them personally." He did, and all five made significant donations.

After four years in the Navy in the civil engineering corps, Lee returned to Charlotte in 1955 with the idea of becoming a civil engineer. Instead, he signed on with Duke for what he thought would just be a short while. Although his credentials were impeccable, he did not want to trade on the family name. When he was given the opportunity to build power plants, he decided to stay, although for years he would not even allow a picture of his grandfather in his office. "I wanted to design and build the best power plants in the world," he once said, "not because I desired promotion but because I wanted to design the best."

He liked the "best." He liked being the best, he liked winning, and he thought that competing in the arena was invigorating. Competition was one of his great bywords. On one occasion, when speaking of the crisis in education in this country, he reminded his audience of the motivating power of competition: "Unless educators feel the hot breath of competition on their necks, like business does, they're not going to manage the enterprise as efficiently and effectively as they must."

Building nuclear power plants in the mid-fifties was not an easy task. The horrific images of Hiroshima still seared the mind's eye. Radiation was a thing to be feared. In an age of wondrous technology, electronic push-button household appliances, tail-finned gadget-equipped cars, and rockets in space, there was a fearful dread of nuclear destruction. Popular culture itself was awash with paranoia fed by "duck and cover" Cold War rhetoric, and Hollywood capitalized on the fear with a cycle of radiation-monster films. In *Them* (1954), ants are transformed into giant predators and roam the Arizona desert. Grasshoppers suffer the same fate in 1957's *The Beginning of the End*, as do spiders in *Tarantula* (1955). Prehistoric beasts emerge from the ocean depths after A-bomb tests and humans are enlarged (*The Amazing Colossal Man*, 1955) or shrunk (*The Incredible Shrinking Man*, 1957), after exposure to atomic radiation.

But horrible atomic power could be tamed and turned to good—that was Bill Lee's conviction. And he would do the taming and the turning. By 1963 Lee had brought on line the first nuclear power plant in the southeast at Pharr, South Carolina.

It took guts, determination, and incredible confidence in one's vision for Bill Lee to proceed as he did with the building of nuclear power plants. But Lee saw the need, and he was aware that he had to educate the public both about that need and about the safety of nuclear energy. In a 1990 speech at the "Emerging Issues Forum" at North Carolina State University, Lee told his audience:

> To achieve the aspired worldwide standard of living of $10,000 annual income per person it will require 0.3-kilo-watt hour electricity input per dollar, or 3,261 kilowatt hours per person per year for the nine billion people on this planet. Thus, in the year 2040, 29.3 trillion kilowatt hours will be needed annually, up from the 9.9 trillion today. When today's students are my age the world must produce about three times as much electricity as today. Present power plants will be worn out in less than fifty years. So, to generate three times as much as today's electricity will mean that these power plants must be replaced by new ones, and their generating capacity must be duplicated with more new plants, then duplicated again.
>
> How will we make that much electricity? With the knowledge we have today we must not abandon any means of generating electricity, nor should we put all our eggs in one basket. To keep all our options open, we should continue with a diverse mix, further developing each of the technologies and lessening the impact on the environment in our quest for optimum solutions. . . . Nuclear-generated electric-

ity will play a much greater role, and this is already evident in some countries but opposed in others. In my view we cannot hope to significantly increase the standard of living of the world's growing population without a substantial contribution from nuclear fission.

It is clear that Lee understood that he had to be a diplomat and a teacher as well as an engineer. In fact, like Rupp, like Eckerd, Bill Lee was a born teacher *and* learner. His daughter Lisa recalls, "He was a good listener and was eager to learn. He listened to criticism without being defensive, but if you were wrong on the facts, he would educate you."

I recall one time when he was being criticized by church members who were wary of nuclear power, and he told me, "Billy, they don't understand. I need to teach them." Many times on Saturday mornings I saw him in the Queens board room with a group of concerned citizens explaining the necessity and wisdom of nuclear power.

Bill Lee was a leader, and teacher, who insisted on staying very close to his people. In one of my very first meetings with Bill as chairman of the Queens board, he told me one of his favorite stories. He began by saying, "You're coming to Queens as a 'hot shot' with a reputation for making quick decisions and taking fast action, but listen to this story: Once, on his first day on the front lines, a spit-and-polish young Marine lieutenant gave his men a rousing pep talk, then charged forward a hundred yards and turned to look at his troops. They were standing still. 'Follow me!' he yelled. And still they stood. They could barely hear him. He was too far away. One young Marine turned to the other and asked, 'What's that damn fool doing out there by himself?' The more experienced sergeant huddled with his men, explained the mission, and then eye-to-eye with them said, calmly, 'Let's go.' They moved forward as a unit in close formation."

"Never get out too far ahead of your troops," Bill Lee told me. "Stay connected, and they will follow you anywhere."

Bill Lee was a wise and master teacher.

Lee probably learned this valuable lesson about communication when he was called to help clean up the radiation leak at Three Mile Island in March 1979, a disaster that he committed to turning into "a docile baby." He was so intent on the task at hand that he prohibited the workers from talking with the media. This, he later admitted, was probably a mistake, a missed opportunity to educate the people about the benefits and the risks of nuclear energy. But, he did help form the Institute of Nuclear Power Operators that he chaired from 1979 to 1982. The industry, Lee believed, must regulate itself by raising the standards of performance and adhering to them. When the Chernobyl accident occurred in April 1986, the nuclear energy industry was dealt another severe blow. Lee immediately rose to the occasion. He recognized that the entire international industry was dependent upon the safety of the weakest link. He therefore urged the world's nuclear providers to band together and adhere to standards of self-regulation. The result was the World Association of Nuclear Operators, which he served as president in 1989.

Lee believed that more energy would make the world a better place, and that nuclear energy was the energy of the future. But yes, he'd add fervently, it had to be made absolutely safe. Once, he was speaking with Martin Palous, chief advisor to then-Czechoslovakia President Vaclav Havel. Palous, whom I had met earlier in Prague during a visit with a Queens study tour, was in Charlotte to speak at an international forum at Queens. When I told Bill Lee about Palous's visit he immediately asked to see him. I took Palous to Lee's office for the visit. What unfolded was unbelievable: Lee had a map of Czechoslovakia with pins identifying all of the country's nuclear plants. In a friendly, professional way, Lee proceeded to describe to Palous the nature of each facility, its age, how it was structured, and the threats it faced in breakdown. He asked Palous to convey to President Havel his best wishes and pledged to come to Czechoslovakia if ever needed.

Palous, himself a teacher, told me afterwards that Lee's performance was absolutely stunning.

From these events and Bill Lee's reaction to them, I learned that good leadership is dependent upon clarity of vision and decisiveness of action. Bill Lee was convinced of the necessity of nuclear power for the future well-being of all life on Planet Earth. He knew that the issue was global and demanded international cooperation and understanding. As an engineer, he knew the facts of the industry, and he had the incisive mind to see the whole as greater than the sum of the parts. As a humanitarian, he knew the fears of the people and the need for convincing explanations, education, and a sensitivity to the needs of his audience. Bill Lee was a man who could translate his thought into decisive action. And he could muster a loyal band of followers through the force of his personality and the clarity of his vision.

But Lee's vision and leadership were not limited to the nuclear power industry. He was a staunch supporter of education and spoke often about the need for improving educational facilities and the public's attitude toward educators. Our future, he believed, will only be as bright as our children are. And local business has a vested interest in making our schools worthy of that future. Speaking on "Competition and the Classroom" before the Rutherford County Industrial Association in 1988, Lee said:

> I applaud your efforts in the local schools and urge you to continue looking for innovative ways to help our future employees. You and I have the privilege and the responsibility of being leaders. Our decisions affect not only the welfare of our businesses but also of our communities. That means we have to start working now to ensure a better-educated workforce in our state. Our companies can only be as good as our employees. Business and industry in every community must play a proactive role in the schools. We have to share our time, our talent, and our expertise. Duke Power employees have gotten involved in their local schools through our "Power In Education" Program, which we launched in 1984. We now have more than 2,100 PIE volunteers involved in educational activities throughout our service area, activities ranging from tutoring to repairing a school boiler.

As leader of the North Carolina Citizens for Business and Industry, Bill Lee was instrumental in forging connections between the corporate sector and educational institutions in a locality. William Friday, former president of the University of North Carolina System, reports the following:

When Bill Lee was the leader of the N.C. Citizens for Business and Industry he became concerned about the quality of public education—schools, community colleges, and the University—in our state. He asked if I would make the principal address [of the meeting] one of defining the major stresses on the system and preparing alternative solutions. He arranged for group discussions following lunch, and the conversations of the day put the business leadership of North Carolina into the debate on public education in a major way. It was his initiative to define for the first time a serious commitment by business and industry to be in partnership with the public schools and public higher education.

A year after Bill Lee's death, at a Heart Ball in his honor, William Grigg, Lee's successor, recalled in his remarks that Lee was once asked what he would like to be remembered for. Griggs quoted Lee as saying, "I would like to be remembered as a person who helped others achieve more than they could have done without me."

Grigg shares another story that captures Lee's essence: At Princeton, Lee was a member of a rowing crew. Following several matches in England, the team embarked on a tour of Europe ending in Paris. During a stop in Switzerland, Lee sighted the Matterhorn. He promptly announced that he planned to forgo the joys of Paris and climb the famous mountain. He hired a guide who schooled him in mountain climbing and then he scaled the peak. Grigg's comment is on target: "That's Bill Lee, find a mountain and climb it."

The list of those Bill Lee helped in his many years of service to the Charlotte community would be long indeed and includes the United Way, the Chamber of Commerce, the Charlotte-Mecklenburg Arts & Science Council, the Presbyterian Church, and the Blumenthal Center for the Performing Arts. And, of course, Queens.

Charities, councils, and boards were not the only ones who could rely on Bill Lee for support. Lee was a patriot. He believed that he had a moral duty to give back to his community. He believed that he had a moral duty to build the Kingdom. He believed that he had a moral duty to make his hometown, his state, his nation, and indeed the world, a fairer, kinder, and more just place. Am I exaggerating? Not at all.

For instance, Bill Lee was also a champion of civil rights. Shortly after he became chairman at Duke, he began moving women and African-Americans into positions of power in the corporation. He promised that 25 percent of Duke officers would be women and one-third of all promotions would go to women and minorities. Lisa Lee recalls him saying, "How could any wise businessperson exclude 50 percent of the job pool? Equality is not only moral and just, it makes good business sense."

Lee was pursuing the same sense of justice when he was hosting the CEO of a major Fortune 500 company, who happened to be Jewish, at a reception at the Charlotte Country Club. The club did not then admit Jews to membership, and Lee said he would not attend if the club would not admit Jews as members. In fact, he went on to say, with considerable heat, that he would resign his membership if the club did not change its policy. Immediately. The club complied. Bill always said that you ought to act out of conviction, not out of fear. "Doing the good thing is always the right thing to do," he often said.

"And *vice versa*."

I remember a time in the late eighties when black students at Queens raised serious concerns about the way the school treated minorities. They didn't feel, they said to me, that the college recognized their importance and their contributions; they didn't always feel accepted as full members of the Queens community, and they didn't like it one bit. One young woman added that there simply weren't enough black students or teachers on campus. If Queens really was an open school, committed to opportunity and diversity, where were the black students and teachers?

I discussed their concerns with Chairman Lee. He said, "Well, let's deal with this directly. We'll invite the students to speak to the board." And so, at the next board of trustees meeting, a group of seven black students were invited to join the trustees. It was a little tense. The seven students were nervous and somber.

Chairman Lee welcomed the students and asked the young woman acting as their leader to introduce each student, along with his or her hometown and intended major. The students then presented their concerns. A discussion followed; everyone was anxious. It's said that Americans have a shockingly hard time talking openly about race, and the trustees and the students were in that sense typical Americans. When the discussion ended, Chairman Lee stood at the door as the students left, thanked each student by name, hugged and shook hands with them, and said, "We love you, and we will do better. You all are great. Let's work together on this."

The next morning one student called me with thanks. She commented on Bill Lee's sincerity and openness. And we did do better. Chairman Lee directed me to formulate a responsible college policy to deal with the issues, and to keep the trustees and students "in the loop."

Born into a famous local family, educated at prep schools and at an Ivy League university, brilliant and wealthy, Bill Lee was always a man of the people. He had a grace and charm and humor about him that appealed to everyone. Here's a favorite Bill Lee story: Once when Lee was taking a group of Soviet scientists on a tour of the McGuire Nuclear Power Plant, one of the visitors admired Lee's cell phone. It was in the late eighties, and cell phones were new at the time. One scientist brought out his cell phone and said he could talk to Moscow from his country house in Minx. Lee turned his phone on and said, "I can talk to Moscow, too." He then punched in the number the scientist gave him and the sexy voice of the Russian's mistress purred "Da" through the receiver.

Bill Lee prized loyalty. He felt it important to "buy American," not because he was a chauvinist, but because he wanted to help fellow Americans. He drove a Chevrolet Impala, not a high-end car, and certainly not a foreign one. He was in the electricity business, and so his home energy was, of course, electricity. In fact, he would not let members of his family use gas in their homes. He planned the Lake Norman housing development, where he and his family had homes, without gas lines. His son States Lee and his wife enjoy cooking and prefer the control one has with a gas burner on a stove. "No way," his father told him, "not in a house next to mine." States worried that if he used a propane tank his father would take a shotgun and shoot it. States and his wife backed down and went all electric in their home.

A few years later, Lisa Lee and her husband Alan Morgan moved back to charlotte from New York, and her father told them that could not have gas in their home either. However, Lisa and Alan compromised and bought a stove with electric burners and a gas grill. Lee acquiesced, but stuck to his guns. "Gas cooking is not as good as electric cooking," he maintained. "Our sales people tell me that."

He was in some ways a very simple man. He was at ease with ordinary people. He was also at ease with the movers and shakers of the world. He was one himself. He had a simple philosophy of life that he passed on to his children: "Figure out what you love to do, and then figure out how to get paid for it." He was never enamored of social position or status or material possessions. These things came to him because of his quality of leadership and the successes he enjoyed by being the very best at what he did, by thinking things through and taking decisive action, by doing the good thing which is the right thing to do. He advised his children to take the time to discover where they can be most useful. Join the small groups, he advised. Do the hard things. Work with the people who really need you. For Bill Lee that was the right thing to do.

But, let me tell you one more thing about Bill Lee, the thing that was the very bedrock of who he was and what he did.

Bill Lee had, I think, an internal compass that pointed not north and south but right and wrong. A fiercely competitive businessman, a master builder, Bill Lee was guided not by the laws of the jungle but by that finely tuned moral compass. He believed not simply in market prices but fair prices; he believed not just in minimum wages but living wages; he believed not in ownership but in stewardship; not in wealth and power but in justice and loving-kindness. Bill Lee was not an overtly pious man, but he was a deeply spiritual man. If I had to describe the source of the energy that drove him, I'd say without hesitation that his energy was, in the end, spiritual energy.

Bill Lee was a man easy to love. He died suddenly and unexpectedly in 1996—we were all stunned. He had been the very explosive incarnation of life energy. But, then again, he died the way he lived, quickly, decisively, with all his wits about him, and I can imagine him saying, with that big smile and an extended hand, to the angel sent to collect him, "Well, let's do it!"

At his funeral, as the *Charlotte Observer* reported, "all had a Bill Lee story." Here's one of my favorites: Once, walking through an airport with a group of Russian scientists, Lee received a strange request. One of the scientists asked to see a church so he could talk to God. He then asked Lee how he talked to God. In the middle of the airport, Bill Lee—corporate CEO, chair of our board of trustees, director of a score of civic groups, brilliant, wealthy, and powerful—promptly fell to his knees and recited the Lord's Prayer.

Bill Lee's daughter, Lisa Lee Morgan, read this moving poem at her father's funeral:

Star-Spangled Man

Star-spangled man, no mere planet
But a sun, a body fused
By Proteus, Self-generating source of power,
Shining light, hour on hour,
Rush! Wind, water, coal, and coil,

Quick! Split the atom, fuse the soil
Don't ever stop, embrace the toil.
Christ-man, His disciple loyal.
Blue eyes blazed like shooting stars
Beneath the lightning brows of Zeus
They let us know we had his attention,
(For better or worse I'll mention)
Lover, hunter, father, friend,
Bully, preacher, Charlotte's kin.
Forgive us for we know not how
To tread the steps he's led 'til now.
This warrior stood to lead the fight
Against the dying of the light.
The closing mind, the fading hope,
The grasping hand, could find no grope
In Bill Lee's camp upon the lake
Where children frolic, swim and play.
He was our star, bright gravity
Round whom we danced 'til God took Lee.

Asked how her boss might react to all this fuss, his longtime secretary Phyllis Simpson said that he'd probably respond with one of his typical sayings: "You honor me beyond my deserving." She's right. But, I think this time I'd disagree with my old board chairman and say, "Mr. Chairman, quintessential servant leader, we haven't honored you nearly enough."

Bill Lee: The Ever-Cheerful Optimist

Hugh McColl

4

HUGH MCCOLL:
A MAN FOR ALL SEASONS

"A leader like Hugh McColl comes along every hundred years, if you're lucky."

—ROLFE NEILL
FORMER PUBLISHER, *The Charlotte Observer*

"He was eager, his people were ready—the result was a brilliant deal for his bank."

—WILLIAM SIEDMAN
FORMER CHAIRMAN FDIC

Speaking at an Atlanta prayer breakfast in October 2001, retired Bank of America Chairman and CEO Hugh McColl challenged business executives to "bring more people to the table, help them achieve their aspirations, share our success with them, and teach them to care for themselves. Together, we can make a better America and a better world."

The story of how a young boy from Bennettsville, South Carolina, (population: 10,000), rose to build America's largest bank and at the same time "bring more people to the table," illuminates a penetrating new dimension and insight into the concept of servant leadership. This intriguing story is told in detail by Ross Yockey in his book, *McColl: The Man with America's Money*, published in 2000.

But there is another important ingredient in Hugh McColl's impressive career that is less well known: the degree to which he was instrumental in transforming Charlotte from a small, Southern city into a progressive "can-do city with a soul" and one of America's most vital urban centers. Further, for the last two decades, he has been the driving force in helping what is now Queens University of Charlotte evolve into one of America's most innovative, diversified, and high-quality urban institutions of higher education.

McColl's commitment to his home community and his philosophy of business was outlined in a speech at the University of Kansas in 1998:

> I'll let you in on a little secret. Banking is not my passion for life. Banking, let's just say business, is not an end within itself. It is a means to an end. It is one of the many activities that we all undertake as part of a greater purpose . . . as Roberto Goizueta, Coca-Cola's late chairman, once said, "a dignified quality of life for all of our citizens." . . . I believe there are three groups to which we all belong that create our community: our work, our family, and all the rest of the people who live where we live. And I believe that the success of each of these groups is dependent on the success of the other two; you can't starve one to benefit the other. If you try, they'll all die. (*The Awakening*, Jerry Footlick, p. 73-74).

While not "dying," Queens in the late seventies was in

severe financial straits. McColl knew this. But how he became a Queens trustee in 1983 and then chairman in 1991 had its genesis in a fateful meeting in 1981 at the Morrocroft Condominiums, home of Queens trustee and longtime patron James J. Harris. Others in attendance were then-Queens chairman Joseph W. Grier and Queens trustee Bill Lee. I was there as Queens's current president. Significantly, none of these Queens trustees was a graduate of the college—it was all-female at the time—and none had any family members who attended the college. But they all shared a common commitment: They were determined to see Queens through its current difficulties and get the college back on a sound course for the future.

A brief profile of each is instructive:

- Joe Grier, a Charlotte native, graduated from the University of North Carolina at Chapel Hill and went on for a law degree at Harvard. His interest in Queens was its connection to the Presbyterian Church and its location in southeast Charlotte. The faculty credits Joe Grier's optimistic attitude and leadership with holding the college together during the rough days of the early 1970s. They especially appreciated his commitment to the library.

- Bill Lee, Duke Power executive and grandson of one of its founders, was also a Charlotte native. He attended Woodbury Forest Prep School in Virginia and then Princeton, where he earned a degree in engineering. His commitment to Queens was due to its being in the neighborhood, its Presbyterian connection, and its commitment to women.

- James Harris, a graduate of the University of Georgia,

was an insurance executive and owner of the enormously successful James J. Harris Insurance Agency. "Mr. Jimmie" married Angelia, the daughter of the late governor of North Carolina, Cameron Morrison. The Morrison and Harris families are longtime supporters of Queens. Angelia Morrison Harris, during her tenure as a Queens trustee, would take "groceries to the Queens girls on the weekend so they would not go hungry." Harris's children Sara and Johnny continued on the Queens board. And son-in-law Smoky Bissell, Sara's husband, led a $10 million drive for Queens that raised $12 million.

I share these profiles because they reveal the degree to which prominent Charlotteans care about Queens. The nurturing culture that made it possible for Queens to achieve its current strong academic position is manifested in these three powerful individuals. When Hugh McColl signed on to join this culture, Queens's future took on a new sense of hope.

Back to the meeting—caring and a sense of urgency were the driving motives behind it. We gathered around a table in the elegance of one of Charlotte's premier homes. Joe Grier began the meeting by stating he felt his time as chairman was up. He had served faithfully as chairman since the early seventies and still cared about Queens, pledging to stay involved, but Queens needed fresh board leadership. He moved right to the point by asking Jimmie Harris if he would assume the chairmanship. Harris restated his commitment to and affection for Queens, but raised his health and age as possible obstacles to his serving. Both Grier and Lee indicated that they did not see these issues as barriers. Then Harris proposed a brilliant solution.

I can see him now, with that lanky frame and courtly Southern manner and in that disarming drawl, turning to Bill Lee and asking slowly, but with a winsome, unmistakable moral earnestness, "Bill, if I do this, will you be my top lieutenant? If you will help me, I will agree to serve for a few years." Harris continued, "Also, Bill, when I can no longer serve, I want you to become chairman. This will ensure continuity." Then he turned to me and said, "Billy, we have high hopes for Queens, and we want to help you achieve them."

All eyes turned to Lee. Rubbing his hands together vigorously and then wiping his brow, and leaning forward with eyes dancing, Lee responded strongly, "Mr. Jimmie, it will be an honor to serve with you. I agree that Queens is on the move, and we must give Billy our full support. And I agree to become chairman when you step down."

Before we adjourned to another room for a celebration with stiff spirits, Jimmie Harris then made another proposal that was to loom large in Queens's future. "Bill, when you step down, we must get Hugh McColl to succeed you. He is heir-apparent at NCNB and is going to be a strong force in Charlotte and the country. He is also young and a Presbyterian." We all agreed that this was a splendid idea, and then we enjoyed a happy celebration.

In 1959, at age twenty-four, Hugh McColl joined American Commercial Trust, a very respectable but unquestionably regional bank. He rose rapidly, and by the early 1970s was one of North Carolina National Bank's up and coming leaders. In 1973, at age thirty-eight, he was in a meeting with NCNB colleague Luther Hodges when another associate, Bill Dougherty, apprised them of an opportunity to buy a little trust company in Orlando, Florida.

"How much money is it losing?" asked McColl.

"No, it's not that," responded Dougherty. It seems that his friend from Pittsburgh National Bank forgot to ask his board if he could buy it and now they wanted him to get rid of it. As luck would have it, NCNB could buy the bank at cost if they wanted it.

McColl and Hodges exchanged glances. "Why not?" asked McColl. "Sure!" was Hodges's answer. Though NCNB's chief executive, Tom Storrs, was out of town, the trust company was immediately purchased. Disney World boomed, Florida became America's hottest growth market, and the rest is history.

"That was the beginning of Bank of America," McColl told me. "Nothing else would have happened without it."

That 1973 purchase was a portent of dramatic things to come. In 1988, McColl, now NCNB's leader, acquired the near-bankrupt $32-billion First Republic Bank in Texas. With about $28 billion in assets, NCNB was an unlikely choice to bail out Republic Bank. Nevertheless, it happened, and NCNB was transformed into NationsBank.

William Seidman, chairman of the FDIC at the time, explains why McColl succeeded. "He was eager, his people were ready. . . . You have to give McColl credit. He stuck with it, and the result was a brilliant deal for his bank . . . NationsBank has been prepared for its opportunities from the beginning."

I once asked McColl about his lightning purchase of Texas's First Republic. He got a call that the deal was possible, and, he told me with a grin, "The sound from the first call about Republic Bank was still hanging in the air as I made the second call." Visionary leaders instinctively sense an opportune moment.

A lot more was to come. Today, NationsBank has become Bank of America, the biggest consumer bank in the nation. McColl's bank grew from $12 billion in 1983 to $966 billion today. After eighty-one acquisitions, by 2001 McColl had become the best-known banker in America and perhaps the world.

McColl's world reach came home to me convincingly during one of my trips to Manila in the early 1990s. I was visiting my friend Jovito Salonga, president of the Philippine Senate, who was thinking about running for the Philippine presidency. (He did run and lost to Fidel Ramos.) Following my meeting with the Senator, I was relaxing in the lobby of the Manila Hotel—where Douglas McArthur lived during World War II—and reading the international edition of *USA Today.* A headline in the business section read, "Aggressive NCNB acquires another bank."

I said to myself in audible tones, "Hugh, you did it again!" Astonishingly, a keen of hearing Pakistani gentleman next to me asked, "Do you know Hugh McColl?"

"Yes," I responded, "he is chairman of the board of the college where I am president. How do you know of McColl?"

He said, "I don't know him personally, but I am a banker, and he is the most astute banker in the world."

Hugh McColl would be the first to argue that he has had a lot of help, but it is widely acknowledged that he has been both the inspirational spirit and driving force behind Bank of America's and Charlotte's meteoric rise to international stature. Throughout its history Charlotte has been driven by economic development. Hugh McColl took on the task of continuing that tradition.

Standing majestically in the heart of Uptown Charlotte is the sixty-floor headquarters of the Bank of America—affectionately dubbed "The Taj McColl." In the surrounding area is a pulsating collage of commercial businesses, restaurants, art centers and museums, and increasingly, a lively neighborhood of residences. This bustling combination of working, living, relaxing, and learning is in sharp contrast to the dead Uptown area of a decade ago. People looked to McColl for leadership, and he invariably delivered. Queens benefited handsomely from the trust that McColl engendered: He has been directly responsible for building a very strong board of trustees, and is personally responsible for generating $40 million plus in gifts for the university. I recall a comment by Pauline Lewis Hayworth that summarizes the respect people have for McColl's leadership and business acumen. Mrs. Hayworth, a Queens graduate, had just agreed to a $5 million contribution to her alma mater. One of Queens's colleges, the Pauline Lewis Hayworth College, now bears her name. After I had thanked her, she stated: "Queens has been in trouble, and as a graduate, I have been worried about its future. The college has a bright future now because with Hugh McColl's involvement, I know it will succeed. He doesn't associate with losers."

Hugh McColl is a confident man who loves action. Once, after he'd retired, I caught him in his study at home before he left on a Texas hunting trip. A gleaming sun, shining through the window, warmed his demeanor: trim and buoyant, he was outfitted in blue jeans, a black sweatshirt, and cowboy boots.

I asked him where his energy came from. "It's instinctive," he said. "I have always had a sense of manifest destiny."

He talked for a moment about his bank's swirl of acquisitions and explosive growth. "In all our acquisitions, I have tried to seize the moment. I have always been confident in my own abilities and judgment."

Bank of America has its own miniature air force, and on the wall of the bank's main hangar at Charlotte-Douglas International Airport is a quote that epitomizes Hugh McColl's approach to life and living:

> Every morning in Africa, a gazelle wakes up. It knows that it must run faster than the fastest lion or be killed. Every morning, a lion wakes up. It knows that it must outrun the slowest gazelle or starve. It doesn't matter whether you are a lion or a gazelle. When the sun comes up, you'd better be running.

After my 1978 introductory meeting with him, Hugh McColl had become a Queens sympathizer, but he didn't become actively involved until 1983, following the 1981 meeting mentioned earlier with Jimmie Harris, Bill Lee, and Joe Grier. That year Chairman Harris called McColl to ask if he would see Bill Lee and me.

When we met, Lee moved quickly to the point: "Hugh, we need you on the Queens board. The college is in your neighborhood, and it's important to Charlotte. Further, it is an institution of the Presbyterian Church. We want you to join us. We need you."

McColl's response was not enthusiastic. "I am on too many

boards now. My experience is that church and college boards don't do much except talk and plan. They don't ever act!"

"That may be true," Lee agreed, "but I promise you things will be different at Queens. Give us a chance."

McColl was mildly intrigued. Leaning forward, with right index finger pointing for emphasis, he announced, "Fair enough. I'll come to one board meeting, but won't speak. I'll listen, and then decide if you all are different."

"That's terrific!" Lee exclaimed. "Thank you, Hugh. We're honored."

"Let's see what happens," is all that McColl would say.

The Queens board room in Burwell Hall filled slowly for the 1983 spring board meeting. Aging window air conditioning units whined annoyingly in the background. Hugh McColl slipped in quietly, sat down, removed his coat, and retrieved a writing pad from his briefcase. Bill Lee and I exchanged approving and hopeful glances, and Chairman Harris then welcomed all to the board meeting, especially prospective member Hugh McColl. McColl smiled a big smile, waved a thank-you, and the meeting proceeded.

The first agenda item was Queens's $2 million operating debt left over from the rough days in the early 1970s. I noticed that McColl was taking notes furiously. After about twenty minutes, he raised his hand and asked if he could make a point. "By all means," Chairman Harris responded. McColl then observed that the debt was sapping critical operating support from the principal purpose of Queens, which was to educate students. Thus, the debt was standing in the way of Queens achieving its full potential. He had a bold idea: What would the board think about him convening a group of Charlotte business leaders in a series of meetings at NCNB, at which time he would offer to loan money to them or their companies at a favorable rate, if they would apply the proceeds to Queens's debt? Those participating would get a tax deduction, and Queens would eliminate a major obstacle to its future. Furthermore, the interest paid on the loan would be tax-deductible.

Spontaneous applause broke out. McColl smiled broadly and, again, waved appreciatively to the board.

This was from a man of action who had agreed to attend *one* meeting to determine if Queens was just going to talk and plan or would be proactive and do something. Within twenty minutes, he had hatched a plan of action that launched the college into a new era. Longtime Queens trustee and Charlotte manufacturing executive Jim Barnhardt captured the significance of the moment: "Queens has just turned a corner."

McColl followed through and convened three debt-elimination luncheons on the fortieth floor of NCNB, one of Charlotte's most prestigious corporate watering holes. He made the pitch, and I followed with the urgency of this move for Queens's future. Bill Lee concluded with an appeal to Charlotte's pride and preserving community tradition. McColl's idea worked: Queens's $2 million debt was eliminated, thus freeing roughly $150,000 per year from the college's operating budget to support its primary mission of educating students.

As I was leaving that meeting, a gentleman indicated that he was giving $25,000 to the cause. I thanked him and asked if he would like to come out to the college for a visit. He thought that sounded like a good idea, and then asked, "Where is Queens, by the way?" I asked why, if he didn't know much about Queens, he would make such a generous donation to us. His response was most revealing: "I came to the meeting because Hugh McColl asked me. I am relatively new to Charlotte, but I know he is a big player, and it is good for me to be in that loop."

In 1991, Hugh McColl succeeded Bill Lee as chairman of the Queens board of trustees. When McColl agreed to chair the Queens board, we decided to continue the practice in which the chairman and the president meet periodically to review college business. Lee once said to me, "Billy, I don't want emergency calls about Queens, and neither do I want to learn in the paper what is going on at the college." McColl was similarly minded and emphasized that these meetings should focus on *actionable items*, especially those that would give the college financial stability and momentum. We met every ten days or so at McColl's home at 7:30 A.M.

On the muggy, overcast morning of August 5, 1991, I left the President's Home at approximately 7:22 for one of our meetings. The Dow Jones Industrial Average stood at an all-time high of 3,169, so I hoped the chairman would be in a good mood. The distance to McColl's house, which I had measured some months ago, was 1.4 miles and took approximately five minutes by car. I wanted to be right on time as I had two very important actionable items. I pulled up to the back of the house at 7:30 A.M. on the dot, knocked on the door, and McColl let me in. He was barefooted, wearing cutoff blue jeans and a black T-shirt. We shook hands and exchanged good mornings. He asked, with certain impatience, if I wanted coffee. "Yes, please," I replied. Coffee in hand, we then got right down to business.

"It's your meeting," he said with a wave of his hand. "What's the agenda for today?"

"Two things, Mr. Chairman. We want Ross Perot to speak at Spring Convocation and receive an honorary degree. Also, we want University of North Carolina President Dick Spangler (who had received a Queens honorary degree earlier) to speak at Commencement the first Saturday in May."

McColl took notes, as he is a copious note-taker. He reminded me that Perot was thinking about running for president in 1992; further, Perot's company had a business relationship with NCNB. Spangler, he pointed out, was a major stockholder at the bank. Both were long shots, we agreed, but he would do what he could. "Anything else?" he asked.

"No," I responded. "Those are two big ones, and I appreciate your help."

He walked me to the door, we shook hands, and I left. My car clock recorded the time as 7:53 A.M.

Fast forward to 9:50 A.M. The phone in my office rang. I answered with, "Bill Wireman."

A stern Marine's voice responded, "This is Hugh McColl. You know those two items you asked me to look into?"

"Yes, sir."

"Well, both have agreed to do what we asked. Confirm the dates with them directly and send me a copy."

"Will do!" I responded eagerly. "This is terrific. Thanks! This is excellent work, Mr. Chairman."

"You're welcome." Click. End of conversation.

Time: 9:53 A.M.

One thing puzzled me about Hugh McColl.

LESSONS FROM THE BIG GUYS

Why would he help me? Why would the chair of a billion-dollar international corporation worry about the fate of a struggling liberal arts college?

He loves action and competition, and maybe it was the challenge. McColl loves puzzles, the more complicated the better, and maybe he saw us as a puzzle to be solved. But over the years McColl has devoted endless hours and a series of extraordinarily generous gifts to Queens. Why? I think there is more to it than simply the challenge. I think there is much more to Hugh McColl than the fearsome man of action. As I got to know him better, I began to see very different Hugh McColls.

Once, Frank Gentry, one of McColl's top lieutenants, told me a story about one of these other Hugh McColls. It was in the mid-1980s. He and McColl were in Washington visiting bank regulators, when McColl looked at his watch and said, "I've got an important call to make."

It was one of these routine team-building gestures every leader has to take. A bank employee in South Carolina was retiring after thirty years of service. McColl wanted to call and congratulate her. They chatted pleasantly, and when he mentioned her thirty years of service, she said, "Actually, it should be thirty-three years, but I had to resign when I stayed home with my first child and never got credit for those years after I came back to the bank."

Hugh McColl responded instantly and said, "Well, you have credit for them now!" He grinned at Gentry and said, "I was ambushed on that one."

He next called Chuck Cooley, his chief personnel officer, to tell him what he had just done, and asked him to research what it would cost to give credit to all women who were in similar situations before maternity leave was standard. Within months, the bank had a new policy. Shrewd public relations? Of course. There's more than a little politician in Hugh McColl. But more than that was at work. McColl has a deeply entrenched concern for rightness and wrongness, an almost physical sensitivity to both. Something isn't right because he wills it; he tries to will, or act on, something because it's right.

Another example: In 1995, McColl was in the midst of the biggest deal of his career. NationsBank had the chance to acquire BankAmerica, and if that amazing event happened, NationsBank-BankAmerica would be one of the biggest banks in the United States, indeed, in the whole world. It was a stress-filled, tension-filled moment. Lives, egos, and billions of dollars were in play. NationsBank was the leader; BankAmerica was the follower. But the BankAmerica executives had cards to play. Among other things, they wanted the new combined corporate headquarters to stay in California, staffed largely with their people. McColl could have agreed. It would have smoothed the road he yearned to go down, and he would have vastly enriched himself personally. All he would have to do would be to abandon his people back in Charlotte. It's done all the time—corporate executives rocketing up in their careers, racking up the latest deal, are not famous for their loyalty to the others who made it happen.

But McColl said no. It was his dream deal; it would make him famous in the business world; he would make millions; all he would have to do was say yes.

But he said no.

"Was that hard?" I asked him recently.

"No, we had come too far to break up our team. I was not about to sell out to BankAmerica for personal power," McColl concluded. "We were determined to stay together. I did the right thing."

Three years later, in 1998, BankAmerica officials came back to the table on McColl's terms. NationsBank merged with BankAmerica in one of the most spectacular business deals in the nation's history. Their joint name would be Bank of America, and the corporate headquarters would stay in Charlotte.

We all know that Hugh McColl and Bank of America made history that day, but what you might not know is this touching story from Hugh's daughter, Jane McColl Lockwood:

"In September 1998, I had just had [my] second child, Luke. Four days after the delivery . . . I was doubled over in pain and could hardly function. I called my parents who live around the corner and told them to come over immediately. They were there quickly, but by that time, I was rolling on the floor in agony. I told my parents I couldn't get through to the doctor, and Dad said, 'We're not waiting on the doctor!' They carried me out to the car and drove me to the emergency room. My dad stayed until he knew I was going to be okay. He then had to go to the biggest board meeting of his career to announce the merger of NationsBank with BankAmerica. This is so typical of my father. Yes, his career was very important to him, but the safety and well-being of his family always came before work."

That's a glimpse of McColl, the family man. Then there is Hugh McColl, not the domineering boss, but the team captain. McColl always insisted, sometimes with great heat, that his people were not his employees, they were his associates. He told me that he had gotten the idea from the chairman of J.C. Penney, and he was immediately convinced that it was right. The point was not only to develop a "team spirit," but to call on everyone in the organization to see themselves—whatever their position—as vital to everyone's success. "The truth is," he told me, "employees work for money; associates work for pride of ownership in the company."

One time, McColl and I were flying to Florida. A young bank consultant joined us on the corporate plane. "What's your task?" McColl inquired. The young man, in his early thirties, responded that he was conducting a study to determine the productivity of the bank's units.

"What's a unit?" asked McColl.

The answer did not please him. It seems that a "unit" is each individual person in the organization. McColl's response was quick and stern: "Don't you dare call my associates units. I do not want to hear that again. They are individuals with families, hopes, and dreams, and each is different and important!" The stunned young consultant apologized and agreed to never use this reference again. It was a long flight to Florida for that young man.

In Bank of America, McColl had some 140,000 "associates," and it's tempting to think that the whole associate business was just public relations. But over the years, again and again, I've spoken with Bank of America people, and without exception, they were devoted to him.

For instance, I was in the lounge atop the Imperial Hotel in Tokyo in the spring of 1999 with some students on a McColl Graduate School Executive MBA study tour after a long day of lectures and interviews. As the group was breaking up, Ricci Bender, a McColl EMBA student and a Bank of America associate, asked if she and her husband, Howard, could join me. "Sure," I responded.

"Dr. Wireman," she began, "I just want you to know how much I am enjoying this trip and how proud I am to be in the McColl School that bears my boss's name." Ricci obviously had great respect for Hugh McColl, and I asked her why. "Because," she said, "Mr. McColl makes us feel we are part of his team. He refers to us as associates—not employees, not workers, not staff, but associates. This makes all of us want to be achievers because if one succeeds, we all win. That makes for a great company spirit. We all feel good about our work and will go the extra mile for him because we know he respects us."

Money is how you keep score in banking, and Hugh McColl dearly loves to win. People and institutions need money to flourish. Both have a responsibility to be good stewards of money. But, oddly enough, I learned that even though he has brought millions to Queens, money is not what America's banker, Hugh McColl, is all about.

McColl was always eager to meet Queens students. One young woman met with McColl, and when I saw her later I asked how the meeting had gone.

"It was great," she enthused.

"Tell me about it," I said.

She had asked McColl to help her get a job. "Why do you want to go into banking?" he inquired.

"I really don't," she responded.

"Then why are you pursuing this route?"

"Because," she admitted, "my parents want me to be in

banking. Bankers make a lot of money."

"What do *you* want to do?" McColl asked.

"Go into the Peace Corps, serve in Africa, and practice my French," she confided.

"Then why don't you do that? The Peace Corps experience will be good background for banking. You can always pursue banking, but you may not have another opportunity with the Peace Corps. You must do what your heart tells you to do! You must have a passion for your work. Think about it and let's talk again."

She followed McColl's advice, entered the Peace Corps in Africa, and today is still doing humanitarian work. We talk now and again, and often she remarks on that decisive meeting with McColl, and his advice about following your heart.

But the most powerful of these other Hugh McColls was Hugh McColl, the good and faithful steward.

Hugh McColl and I are both Presbyterians, and if there is a bedrock Presbyterian ethic, it is stewardship.

This world, and all that is in it, is not ours to own or consume, let alone abuse. This world, and all that is in it, belongs to the One who created it. We are called to be His stewards. We are to care for this place, this world, protect it and repair it and improve it, and pass it along freely to the next generation of stewards. An odd ethic, maybe, for one of America's greatest capitalists, but it is the ethic, I think, which defines Hugh McColl.

Stewardship meant careful care of other people's money deposited with McColl's banks. Stewardship meant concern not simply for his own career and wealth and power but concern for everyone for whom he worked, and with whom he worked, and who worked for him. Stewardship meant care and concern and active engagement with his community.

That's why, I think, he became so committed to Queens.

And that's why, I think, he has been such a central figure in the Charlotte community.

Looking back, it is this engaged stewardship that inspired me most. Again and again, I witnessed McColl take time from his immense banking responsibilities and devote that time to his community.

McColl is a proud South Carolinian, deeply attached to his home state. When the debate in his native South Carolina was raging over whether the Confederate flag should be removed from the state capitol building in Columbia, McColl marched with the folks who thought it should come down.

In the mid-1990s, McColl read in the *Charlotte Observer* that a provision for public art had been eliminated from the budget for the new police headquarters building. In an effort to save money, City Council had decided to build a functional headquarters and cut any public art elements. But McColl has always believed that part of caring for your beloved community means working hard to make your beloved community lovely. Disagreeing strongly with the city council's move, McColl called several business associates, and by noon, had raised $90,000 to restore this item to the building budget. Hugh McColl's friend, Ben Long, an internationally renowned artist, was subsequently commissioned to add frescoes to the police building. And why did McColl do this? "Police women and men appreciate art as much as others. They work hard, and it is only fair that we provide aesthetically pleasing working conditions for them."

Stewardship means concern and care and loyalty. Steward-ship means being in for the long haul, being together through thick and thin. It means that you don't commit lightly, but that when you commit, you commit wholeheartedly. As McColl often said to me, "If I'm in for a dime, I'm in for a dollar."

McColl stayed with the same bank, in all its various forms, for more than four decades. His father, Hugh Sr., a former banker, taught Hugh Jr. the value of a long-term commitment.

In 1966, young Hugh McColl was making $14,500 per year at American Commercial Bank. His friend, Hootie Johnson, with Bankers Trust of South Carolina, offered him $20,000 and a 15 percent bonus. McColl declined. Johnson persisted: How about $30,000, a 15 percent bonus, and the bank presidency? McColl said no again. However, Johnson wouldn't give up: His next offer was $34,000, the presidency, and a bank directorship.

McColl then asked his daddy for advice.

McColl's father: "Are you and Jane getting along okay?"

Hugh, Jr.: "Yes, sir."

Hugh, Sr.: "Do you need anything?"

Hugh, Jr.: "No, sir."

Father to son: "It's easy to move from a big bank to a little bank, but almost impossible to move from a little bank to a big bank."

Hugh Jr. got the message and declined Johnson's offer. Hugh McColl, Sr., helped remind his son of what he had said shortly after being hired at American Commercial: "Someday, Daddy, I'm gonna run that bank." On this occasion, McColl was "in for a dime" and did what his heart (and his daddy) told him to do.

Hugh McColl has had a similar unshakable commitment to Queens. Working with him, I was struck not only by his uncanny ability to raise money, but even more by his astounding ability to inspire trust.

For example: In the fall of 1994, Florida banker Al Ellis donated $2 million to Queens to name our business school after Hugh McColl. It was Ellis's idea. We had originally gone to Mr. Ellis with the idea of naming the school after himself. He said no. Instead, he said, "Since our merger (*acquired* would be McColl's word), Hugh McColl has made me a lot of money, and he has treated me with sensitivity and respect. He didn't have to do that, you know. I appreciate his many courtesies, and I want to do something for him. I will give you the money if you will name the school after McColl."

Another example: John Sykes is one of America's great entrepreneurs. Sykes jokes that he grew up in Charlotte "on the wrong side of the tracks from Queens." He started his own technology company even before the great tech boom of the 1990s and set up shop in Tampa, Florida, where he became a community leader and $10-million benefactor of the University of Tampa. A quick-thinking Queens trustee and McColl School EMBA graduate, Dee Ray, was living in Tampa, and she and her husband, Rick, not only pointed out to our board that John Sykes was from Charlotte, but had, in fact, attended Queens College in the 1950s, a time when men could take courses but not graduate from the then all-female school.

Dee Ray called McColl immediately and suggested a meeting with Sykes. In typical fashion, McColl sensed an urgent need to "seize the moment" and flew off to Tampa. McColl and Ray met with Sykes. Sykes quickly agreed to make a generous five million contribution to the college; more than that, he became an indefatigable Queens supporter, giving generously of his time and talent.

Why? John Sykes said to me, "When I was starting my business in Charlotte, Hugh McColl's bank made me a loan when everybody else turned me down. He has always been one of my role models, and it is an honor for me to be involved with him and Queens." The John H. Sykes Learning Center is now the home of The McColl Graduate School of Business on the Queens University of Charlotte campus.

McColl's unshakable commitment evokes the same in others. His loyalty, his trust, his respect, not to mention his inexhaustible energy, generate the same qualities in the people around him.

Some of those people who have come to admire McColl as I have are very high profile.

Once, some of the McColl School faculty had the bold idea of inviting former Federal Reserve Board Chairman Paul Volcker to speak at Queens. It was, to say the least, an optimistic. I mentioned the idea to McColl.

To my amazement, I then got a call from New York. From Paul Volcker himself. He said something like this: "Dr. Wireman, I understand you have one of the finest little colleges in the country down there. Hugh McColl tells me that the students in his school want me to speak to them. I would be honored. Let's work out a date."

So yes, Paul Volcker came to Queens. He was most generous with his time and answered numerous questions following his lecture. When the students presented Volcker with a McColl School sweatshirt, he immediately shed his coat and donned the gift. He still had it on as we left him at the gate for his flight back to New York. A waiting passenger asked me if that fellow wasn't Paul Volcker. "Yes," I responded. "Very interesting," the puzzled gentlemen mused. Volcker waved good-bye, and we watched him walk down the ramp with "McColl School of Business" displayed in bold black letters on the back of one of the world's leading financial figures.

Then Bill Gates came to visit.

I received a call from Hugh McColl's chief of staff, Vick Phillips. "Would you," Phillips inquired, "be interested in having Bill Gates speak at Queens?" Gates and McColl were in conversation on a business proposition, and Gates suggested that McColl have dinner with him on his plane at the Charlotte airport on his way back to Redmond, Washington. McColl had a better idea: Why not, McColl asked, speak at a McColl School event and then have dinner later?

It took less than three seconds for me to respond to Vick's inquiry: What can we do and when? Sit tight, Phillips counseled. He would get back in touch with me. Phillips called back: Gates would address a McColl School gathering in the spring, as long as we could promise him that it would not be a crowd of white-haired men in pinstriped suits. He wanted diversity of gender, race, and age.

So, Bill Gates came to visit. The program called for me to introduce McColl who would in turn introduce Gates. We were to meet backstage in our auditorium. Gates arrived promptly on time with an entourage; McColl followed immediately afterwards, alone. As the three of us sat down at a metal-legged table with a cracked wooden top, in uncomfortable straight-back chairs, I couldn't help but think of the contrast between the caliber of the two principals—Bill Gates and Hugh McColl—and the surrounding furnishings. The scene was dark; the walls were stark, gray concrete; and a heavy curtain hung over our heads. And here we had two of the world's most prominent entrepreneurs on the Queens campus chatting in quiet conversational tones about topics ranging from the economy to children. We went on stage. I introduced McColl, he introduced Gates, and Gates made a folksy, thirty-minute speech, which was a combination of video and narrative, to a diversified, packed crowd.

Following the lecture, Gates and McColl attended a reception on campus. There was lots of handshaking and picture-taking. Finally, Bill Gates and Hugh McColl sped off in a long black limousine to have dinner and continue their business discussions. As their car rounded the Burwell Circle curve to exit onto Selwyn Avenue, a McColl School student approached me smiling, thanked me, and declared excitedly the overwhelming sentiments of the crowd, "Dr. Wireman, it just doesn't get any better!"

Why did this happen? Why did Bill Gates speak at Queens? We know the answer: Because an imaginative man-of-action turned a dinner invitation aboard a private jet into a major coup for a small college and a community he cares about deeply.

Hugh McColl retired in April 2001, and there was a grand retirement celebration at the Blumenthal Performing Arts Center in Charlotte. Following the event, I joined a group at a nearby restaurant. Someone in the party repeated retired *Charlotte Observer* publisher Rolfe Neill's remark that "a leader like Hugh McColl comes along every hundred years, if you're lucky." Since I know both Rolfe Neill and Hugh McColl, I was asked if Neill's judgment on McColl was hyperbole. "Rolfe Neill is not given to hyperbole," I responded. Neill's involvement in civic affairs and his weekly Sunday column on the op-ed page of the *Observer* was widely read, respected, and revealed a no-nonsense, tough-minded man with good judgment. After listing McColl's contributions to Charlotte and his success in business, all at the table agreed that Neill was right: Hugh McColl really is unique in the galaxy of civic and business leaders who have given the city its character and conscience.

We all agreed that Hugh McColl was a Man for All Seasons.

Hugh McColl could also be intimidating!

I'll never forget once when he was scheduled to speak to an important group in a large classroom on campus. I had gone over carefully with my staff the logistics: chair arrangements, temperature, microphone volume, and other details. You can guess what happened. When McColl arrived every imaginable thing, and several unimaginable things, went wrong. It was as hot as the inside of an oven, the microphone didn't work, on and on. After surveying the situation, he looked at me with that Marine stare and barked, "Wireman, we have screwed this up every way possible. The only reason we can't screw it up further is that there are no options left!" After we corrected the faults, he put his hand on my shoulder and quietly but firmly declared, "This fiasco is now over. Let's put it behind us and move on." Needless to say, we made sure ever after that things that were supposed to work really did!

But it is not fire and intimidation that I recall from my

years with McColl: It is a distinct kind of leadership. Action-packed, fired with energy, it was leadership that created not simply wealth but trust; not just power but loyalty and care, and yes, love. Its secret was, I think, this: Hugh McColl, the boss, the master entrepreneur, America's banker, the former Marine officer, is in his heart, a steward and a servant, and who, because of that, inspires in the rest of us a deep sense of stewardship and servanthood.

This sense of stewardship and sensitivity was revealed eloquently in a speech McColl delivered to the Governor's Summit on Race, held in Charlotte on February 17, 1999. This speech was so timely and powerful that I submitted it to *Vital Speeches of the Day* (April 15, 1999), which prides itself on sharing "the best thought of the best minds on current national questions." On that occasion McColl said:

> What I want to do is to work together to build communities of justice, equality and hope . . . communities where every man, woman and child—regardless of race—pulls their weight, even as they reach back with a strong hand and a compassionate heart for those—once again, regardless of race—who have been left behind. . . . This is what I am working for. And I look forward to working with all of you to get it done.

Finally, this philosophy of McColl's to act with "a strong hand and compassionate heart" was captured beautifully in an incident I observed on one of those early mornings when I met McColl at his house to review college business. That morning he stepped out of his house to greet me. A burly African-

American man was loading debris from McColl's yard into his pick-up truck. McColl struck up a conversation with the man and asked about his son. He's doing fine, the gentleman responded, and was trying out for the basketball team. McColl immediately retrieved a basketball, gave it to the yard man, and asked this father to give the ball to his son. His instructions said it all: "Tell your son to practice hard and make good grades. This is America, and everyone has a chance." That spirit of caring about a young man, whom he did not know, whose father was a yard man, impressed me greatly.

That servant leadership, as much as the creation of a mammoth bank, is his great achievement.

Conclusion

Dreams and Mentors

Dream no small dreams. They butter no parsnips.

—Anonymous

[The] young . . . need dreams and mentors.

—Gail Sheehy

I t's time to finish the story of my leadership odyssey. And what a rewarding experience it has been.

On July 1, 2002, I retired from the presidency of Queens University of Charlotte. For fifty-two years, beginning in the fall of 1950, with only a four-year interlude which included the Marine Corps, graduate work, and teaching a year at Shepherd College in West Virginia, I have been involved as a student, professor, administrator, or college president in a search for that creative juxtaposition between the life of the mind and the life of the spirit—between faith and reason. The principal settings for this journey have been two Presbyterian colleges: Eckerd College in St. Petersburg and Queens in Charlotte.

By adding to the diversity and strength of American higher education, the United States' seven hundred church-related colleges are precious treasures and contribute significantly to making American colleges and universities collectively the world's best. These church-affiliated institutions speak to the most impoverished area in American colleges and universities: undergraduate, residential, liberal arts education. Because these small institutions are church-related, they have a soul, and thus provide students with a touch of prophecy, which is often absent in larger institutions. It is clearly in the public interest to keep these gems strong and vital.

My life has been an odyssey in leadership on behalf of these very special institutions. I have been carried on this odyssey by winged horses that never tire.

I was given those winged horses by four remarkable teachers: the "master of basketball," Adolph Rupp; the "king of retail," Jack Eckerd; the "man who lit the skies," Bill Lee; and "America's banker," Hugh McColl.

They were my mentors, my masters, my teachers. They helped me achieve my dreams.

What was their key lesson? It's surprising in a way.

Each of these four was a powerhouse, a mighty engine who dominated the world around him. True, they were different in age, temperament, and profession—Rupp, the coach, was born in 1901 and died in 1977; Eckerd, the drug magnate, born in 1913, died in 2004; Lee, the engineer, born in 1929, passed away in 1996; and McColl, the banker, born in 1935, retired from his bank in 2001, but still lives in Charlotte where he heads a number of thriving companies related to investment banking and the arts. All four men had great personal magnetism and somehow seemed to stand taller than anyone nearby.

I remember listening to Hugh McColl address the Board of Visitors of the John Sykes School of Business at the University of Tampa at 8 A.M. on a hot spring day in the late 1990s. Tampa's political and corporate elite was there hoping to get a tidbit about how to be successful in politics or business. What they got instead was pure Hugh McColl: Corporations must be good citizens. The cultural, educational and moral climate in the community is just as important as corporate profits. Together, they make a powerful combination.

He received a loud, sustained, standing ovation. One crusty corporate executive said as he was leaving, "That's not what I expected, but it's a damn relevant message. And he is absolutely right." McColl had told them what they hadn't expected to hear, maybe hadn't even wanted to hear, but by the time he was done, they were ready to march under his banner.

All four of my Big Guys were like that: They were people of such stunning presence that you'd instantly be sure that the secret of their leadership power was their explosive, inexhaustible, titanic egos. You'd be sure that their leadership was all about them.

And you'd be dead wrong.

Here's the shocking thing: In the end, their leadership was not about them at all. Their leadership was sacrificial and self-transcending. Their charismatic power was fired by their amazing ability to go beyond ego and career and self and to tap into energies infinitely more creative than anything found in a single personality.

My teachers achieved heroically because they led self-sacrificially.

My teachers were "servant leaders" and that's how they transformed their worlds.

Now this is not a new phenomenon at all. In fact, it is ancient.

The Romans awarded the laurel wreath to soldiers who risked their lives for others; in Roman legend, the greatest leaders, like Cincinnatus, were great precisely because they risked their lives for the Roman Republic. Jesus insisted that only those willing to lose their lives would save them. The "greatest in the Kingdom" would be those who were the servants—not the masters—of all.

The poet Lord Byron expressed this powerfully in his "Ode to Napoleon Bonaparte." Byron, like Beethoven and many others of that tumultuous generation, had deeply admired Napoleon. Napoleon was undeniably an extraordinary figure, and Byron, Beethoven, and millions of others hoped that Napoleon would use his awesome abilities to mobilize love and create a just society. Instead, Napoleon used his abilities to advance himself and his own inexhaustible ego. In his "Ode," Byron contrasts Napoleon and his tyrannical ego to George Washington. Washington was in some ways Napoleon's inferior. Washington was not a genius; Napoleon was. Washington was a good but not necessarily a great captain; Napoleon was one of the greatest commanders in history. But Washington—precisely because he surrendered his own ego for the good of the Republic—was in the end a greater man than Napoleon, the tyrant. In the end, Byron insists, it was Washington's self-sacrifice that made the greater leader, made Washington "The Cincinnatus of the West," whose memory, Byron wrote, made "men blush that there was but one."

Conclusion: Dreams and Mentors

There need not be just one, though.

Why was Washington greater than Napoleon? Because, as historian Garry Wills explains, Washington had mastered the "art of resignation." Washington had learned that his power was directly proportional to his willingness to sacrifice himself; he had learned that the only creative power is selfless power (Wills, *Cincinnatus*).

So, as I end, I'd like to summarize not some abstract theory of leadership, nor sketch a history of leaders, but rather, in an informal and personal way, pass along to you the lessons I've learned from my four extraordinary teachers regarding what leadership is all about.

To be sure, my four teachers were profoundly different people. Their leadership "styles" were quite different.

One incident with each calls to mind the different styles of these leaders: Infrequently, but often enough to remember, I did something to displease my mentors. The way they reacted embodied the same principle but with a different technique.

Rupp used sarcasm to remind me that the telephone was a great invention and that I should have called him when a prospect's plane was two hours late arriving in Lexington. Then he said, "I don't want to hear about that again."

Eckerd was very unhappy that, following a call from Florida Governor Rubin Askew, I endorsed a corporate profits tax in Florida, without discussing it with him. He made his point in an unmistakably clear and firm way, but then concluded, "In the end you have to do what you think is right, but you still should have told me."

Lee was not pleased about a story that appeared in the

Charlotte Observer about then-North Carolina U.S. Senator Terry Sanford's idea that I should challenge North Carolina Senator Jesse Helms in 1990. First, Lee contended, as did Eckerd, that I should have told him. Then he proceeded to give me strong, fatherly advice about the different demands of politics and a college presidency. "Politics is about money and compromise," Lee pointed out. "Education," he continued, "is about preparing the young for citizenship and service. The second is you, Billy; the first is not."

McColl let me know in no uncertain terms once that we should not have the Queens trustee meeting on Martin Luther King Jr.'s birthday. His bank was closed that day, and he would be "unavailable to attend." Needless to say, we changed the meeting date. On another occasion, he indicated in graphic terms that a presentation to the board by an administrator had been much too long and disjointed. "Shorten the reports and get to the point; we're not here for dissertations" was his sharp instruction.

While I am a couple of years older than McColl, with him as with the other mentors, who were all older than I, I applied the Marine Corps' principle of senior officer and junior officer. I was the junior officer with each of my mentors; thus, I always treated them with deference and respect. My mentors shared, and what I learned from them, were principles of self-sacrificial leadership, servant leadership, the George Washingtonian style of leadership, which alone can lead to genuinely heroic achievement.

Let me outline **nine themes**, which recurred in the lessons of my four teachers. Not all nine themes were typical of each person all the time, of course; some themes were much more prominent in some persons than in others. But, these nine flesh out the heroic, self-sacrificial, leadership typical of them all.

EACH OF MY TEACHERS, to begin with, could be called a **"master of the game."** Each was amazingly skillful at what he did; each had the capacity to lose himself in the sheer sport of what he did. Like great athletes, all four deeply loved what they did, realizing at the very same time that in the end, what they did was a kind of "game" from which they'd need, one day, to step away. Precisely because they could lose themselves in the game, they became masters of the game.

EACH WAS WHAT Theodore Roosevelt, in one of his most famous and popular speeches, called a **"man in the arena."** Speaking at the Sorbonne, in Paris in 1910, Roosevelt argued that:

> It is not the critic who counts, not the man who points out how the strong man stumbled, or where the doer of deeds could have done better. The credit belongs to the man who is actually in the arena; whose face is marred by the dust and sweat and blood; who strives valiantly; who errs and comes short again and again; who knows the great enthusiasms, the great devotions and spends himself in a worthy cause; who at best, knows in the end the triumph of high achievement, and who, at worst, if he fails, at least fails while daring greatly; so that his place shall never be with those cold and timid souls who know neither victory or defeat.

Roosevelt would have admired each of my four teachers. Each had not simply a capacity for action, but a *passion* for action. Each hungered for projects, for adventures, for the next hard task. John Kennedy famously vowed to put a man on the moon "not because it is easy but because it is hard," and each of my teachers thrilled to the kind of challenges Kennedy found so invigorating. It was never their careers that came first, never their personal power and certainly never their personal luxury or safety that mattered, what mattered was the game, and the more challenging the better.

THIRD, EACH WAS a **"master builder,"** not a "courtier." Courtiers are careerists, opportunists, apparatchiks, men and women who find ways to ingratiate themselves to the top, whose chief object of affection is themselves. There are many courtiers in the world. My teachers, though, were not among them. To the contrary, my teachers wanted to build not their careers but their teams, their institutions; their powerful ambitions went far beyond themselves. They wanted to construct a great team, a strong business, something not only big and strong but good. Like Washington, and unlike Napoleon, they wanted to create communities in which others could prosper, communities that would long outlive their founders. Historians have often noted that tyrants confuse their personal biographies with their nations' histories. What's good for them is by definition good for their nations. Genuine heroes elevate their nations' histories over their own biographies. What matters is what Dr. King called the "beloved community," what matters is building a good and just and prosperous world, and that is infinitely more important than "me," no matter how inflated.

Conclusion: dreams and Mentors

EACH OF MY TEACHERS WAS, paradoxically, **rooted** but **restless**. They were driven, without exception, by "the unrest of the yet unmet." Each had a strong sense of identity and self-confidence, rooted in a powerful sense of the past and its role in the present. Each was strongly loyal to his company, his state, his country, his family. It was this rootedness, I think, that enabled them to be so restless, so drawn to the future, so determined to look over the horizon. As loyal to the past as they were, my teachers were never prisoners of the past. In fact, they were not so much propelled forward by the past as drawn forward by the future. Every great leader has a powerful vision of the future, a vision which he or she then incarnates and compellingly conveys to those of us still present-bound. Every great leader is restless, eager to act, to bring this vision of the future into reality. That they themselves might never experience that future reality, that like Moses they might never enter the Promised Land, is in the end irrelevant. What matters is the vision and its realization.

ALL FOUR COULD BE described accurately as "**gestalt visionaries.**" They had an amazing ability to *connect*, to see how past shaped present and present shaped future, to relate foreground to background, the subjective to the objective, the immediate with the long-term, the text with the context, the parts with the whole. Their thinking was never episodic, their vision was never tunnel vision.

This visionary principle came into sharp focus, for example, during the 1986–87 debate in the Queens Task Force charged with ensuring that the college was strategically positioned for the twenty-first century. We were at a critical point and the question was raised as to whether it was wise for Queens, just now regaining its financial footing, to undertake an expensive, risky strategy to go coed, raise faculty and staff salaries 50 percent in five years, add ten new professors, and add an internship and international experience for all students as a part of the tuition. Hugh McColl and Bill Lee were both members of the Task Force. At a critical point in the debate, McColl said to Lee, "Bill, let's excuse ourselves and talk this over," which they did. After thirty minutes, they came back with the verdict: Queens cannot afford **not** to do these things if we are "really serious about the future." They said, "This package will give us a market niche, and we must go for it." Importantly, they both pledged to help raise the money. And they did.

SIXTH, ALL FOUR WERE proud **patriots**, honored to think of themselves as citizens of a great republic. McColl served as a Marine officer, Lee as a Navy officer, and Eckerd was an Air Force pilot (Rupp was too young for service in World War I and too old for World War II). There was nothing boastful or chauvinistic about their service. Instead, all of my teachers insisted on seeing the text of their lives in the context of community and nation. Each had a keen sense of duty, a term we don't often hear today. They felt obligated to make their communities better. To be a citizen meant to be a free individual living in a community with other free individuals. It meant not taking but giving back, not using up but building up. It wasn't enough to be a coach or a business leader; you had to be part of your neighborhood, you had to help pull the wagon, make the decisions, take the heat, serve your community and your nation. This is the essence of servant leadership.

ALL WERE **deeply spiritual men.** McColl, Lee, and Eckerd belonged to the Presbyterian Church. Rupp had a Lutheran background. But, Heaven knows, they weren't saints! Their allegiance to traditional religious practices was sporadic at best. Each had his own faults and weaknesses, and yet each was energized by an intense commitment to nonmaterial, transcendent realities like courage and loyalty, and above all, the reality of love and a concern "for the least of these." The ancient Greeks thought that two forces shaped the universe, love and hate. Love builds up; hate tears down. Love includes; hate excludes. Love exudes hope; hate exudes fear. Love creates; hate kills. All of us, the Greeks thought, are mixtures of love and hate, now driven by one, now by another. But love and hate are not just human attributes, they are invisible realities, indeed the very bases of reality. When I say that each of my teachers was deeply spiritual, I mean not only that they were religious, but that by abandoning themselves, found themselves part of the vast force of love.

EACH WAS **at heart a teacher.** What each wanted to build up, in the end, were persons. They could be fearsome and volcanic to be sure. But at their best they were coaches, mentors, guides, Jedi-masters. They became my teachers because they saw in teaching a way not so much to enrich their own lives as to enrich the lives of others. I was one of the lucky ones whose life was immeasurably enriched by theirs.

One example stands out about McColl's love of teaching. The Marine Corps produced a small book, *Warfighting*, which outlined the Corps' tactics and strategies in winning wars. One Saturday morning, I sat for ninety minutes awed by his presentation to a McColl School EMBA class at Queens, during which he outlined the ways that the Marine strategy for winning on the battlefield could be effectively applied to leadership in business. The students had read the book, and throughout the class McColl peppered them with "What do you think?," "Can you see how this will work for you?", among other penetrating questions. One student commented afterwards that McColl should have been a professor.

FINALLY, FOR EACH OF MY TEACHERS, **leadership was not a "style" but a "way."** Leadership was not something you put on like an old hat, but a committed way of living. Like knights of old, my teachers were committed to a distinctive mode of living, a kind of chivalry, if you will, a way of living grounded in commitment to principle. For my teachers, leadership was not simply a tool to achieve some external end. For them, leadership shaped how they lived, what they valued, what they disdained. We all have lives to spend; what matters is what we spend it on. My teachers taught me to see leadership as a noble way of living that was worth a life.

It's a funny thing. Some people assume that leadership means promoting yourself, surrounding yourself with all the luxurious symbols of status and power, getting all you can get, freeing yourself finally from the laws that govern the rest of us. Isn't that the whole point of leadership? Doesn't leadership ultimately mean that you're the boss; you're not accountable to anyone; you're a law unto yourself; you can shake off the restraints that govern mere mortals? Doesn't leadership mean that you become "godlike," a supreme being who worships no one but is worshiped by all, someone above all laws, all limits, above even mortality?

All of my mentors would have angrily disagreed. Leadership is all about responsibility and accountability, and making people "healthier, wiser, freer." Because you're the boss, you're responsible; you're responsible and accountable to your customers, your employees, your stockholders, your conscience—and as Jack Eckerd increasingly became aware, to God. Put simply, leadership is not an add-on; it is a demanding, but deeply fulfilling, way of life.

Leadership? What my four mentors have taught me is that the biggest obstacle to my being a good leader is me! My career, my agenda, my plans, above all, my ego was the biggest stumbling block I had to overcome. But, by immersing myself in the game, by risking myself in the arena, by building and not simply climbing, by looking beyond myself to both past and future, by locating myself in the great gestalt of the "tides of humanity," by becoming a patriot, and a teacher, and above all, by recognizing the divine in everything I do, I might be able to become a kind of servant leader. And only then could I hope for truly heroic achievement.

Sadly, but importantly, I write in the shadow of September 11, 2001. A lot changed on that terrible day. One thing that finally came to an end, I'm convinced, is a type of leadership rooted in greed, grasping, appetite, self-promotion, and ego—Napoleonic leadership, if you will. Perhaps that sort of leadership was tolerable in the heyday of the roaring 1990s, when the American economy was booming, when the United States was the unchallenged world power, when, we were told, "history," with all its pain, contradictions, and cost, "had ended." Hopefully, what has ended is the likes of Enron, Andersen, Global Crossings, Tyco, and WorldCom. The thousands of innocent and trusting employees of these wayward corporations who lost their jobs and life's savings by being betrayed deserved better. Had the executives who betrayed them been driven by the principle of servant leadership, all of this would have been avoided.

Contrast these "me-first" leaders with the heroes of that awful 2001 September hour. Significantly, these patriot-leaders were not the inside traders who had scored big, not the lobbyists with the golden connections, not those slick people who know how to work the system, not the rich and famous, not the celebrities and glitterati. No, the heroes of that day were the cops and firefighters and emergency medics and all the others who rushed into the inferno, at grave risk to their own lives, to pull others out. These heroes were quickly joined by other men and women who risked their lives in faraway lands to protect the rest of us. These heroes, like my four mentors, are leaders driven by "winged horses that never tire." Theirs is a leadership rooted in servanthood.

It was said of the distinguished British architect, Sir Christopher Wren, who designed London's magnificent St. Paul's Cathedral, among other masterpieces, that if you want to see evidence of his work, "just look about you."

On that principle, my mentors score high.

As well as anyone I know, Hugh McColl understands, in both his intellect and in his senses, the exploding diversity and ethnicity that is driving the world today. His life has been devoted to channeling this potentially destructive explosion into building the largest commercial bank in America, and helping to transform Charlotte into a vital, modern city. In this process, he has practiced the principle of inclusiveness—hundreds of women, minorities, and young people are beneficiaries of McColl's bedrock belief: "This is America. Everyone has a chance."

We are all beneficiaries of the late Duke Power chairman's untiring efforts to make the world safe for nuclear energy. Bill Lee's optimistic, cheerful countenance inspired all who knew him. As one of his admirers put it, "Bill was a brilliant man with a good heart." The World Association of Nuclear Operations and the Institute of Nuclear Power Operators are just two of the monuments to Lee's vision and tenacity in seeking the public good. Additionally, Bill Lee and Hugh McColl respected each other greatly, and they were close allies in Charlotte's meteoric rise in stature.

In addition to revolutionizing the retail drugstore business, Jack Eckerd devoted his life to helping others. His philanthropic commitments saved a struggling Eckerd College to continue on its course to distinction. Twice he offered himself for public office, and his concern for prison reform and wayward children who could not be handled in the traditional welfare programs are living testaments to his servanthood.

From 1930 to 1972, Kentucky's Adolph Rupp built a basketball dynasty that brought pride to a whole state and a whole region. Hundreds of his former players and associates are more competent and effective human beings because of his insistence on excelling, being the best that you can be, and concentrating on fundamentals. Rupp Arena in downtown Lexington fills with twenty-one thousand fans every time Kentucky plays a home game. Rupp's spirit of competition and pride pervades each of these occasions. Further, Rupp's concern for disabled children has brought relief, comfort, and joy to thousands of unfortunate children and their families.

Importantly, these servant leaders were not "flashes in the pan," or in for the short haul. They reflected Hugh McColl's philosophy of, "If I'm in for a dime, I'm in for a dollar." They all stayed with basically one institution for their entire careers. Rupp was with Kentucky for forty-two years, from 1930 to 1972; Eckerd began his career with the family business in 1940 and retired forty-six years later in 1986; Bill Lee worked with Duke Power for thirty-nine years, from 1955 to 1994; and Hugh McColl began work with his bank in 1959 and retired forty-two years later in 2001. Their combined 169 years of service to four institutions stands in counterpoint to the tentativeness and volatility of our time.

These four high achievers represented another principle of servant leadership outlined by Robert Greenleaf: They saw "walls as doors" to be opened for making the world a better place.

They were true servant leaders.

In addition to terrorism, we are now confronted with a brutal war with Iraq, a nuclear and hostile North Korea, and a rupture in the alliance between Europe and America that won the Cold War and kept the peace for fifty years. These challenges have shaken the international community to the bottom of its soul. This struggle has prompted a serious question: Has there ever been a time when we more desperately needed leaders to turn "walls into doors" of opportunity, a leadership that unites rather than divides?

Has there ever been a time when we more desperately needed self-sacrificial, servant leadership?

I think not. These four Big Guys improved the things they touched—they moved beyond wealth and power and influenced civic and moral dimensions of our society for the good of all mankind.

May we do the same.

Acknowledgments

Good writing, my high school English teacher, Mrs. Clayton, reminded us many times, is nothing more than telling an interesting story with passion, conviction, and imagination. To the degree that I have achieved this worthy objective, much of the credit is attributed to many people who added immeasurably to this work. To name a few:

My distinguished Queens colleagues Professor Richard Goode and Professor Robert Whalen helped me more than I describe. This is our fifth collaborative literary effort, and their research, writing, and editing skills and good judgment on sequence, anecdotes, and content get better with each edition. Both are writers and recognized scholars in their fields—Dr. Goode as a Shakespeare and literature expert and Dr. Whalen as a respected scholar of German, Russian, and European history. Master teachers, both have been honored as North Carolina Professor of the Year.

My trusted and exceptionally competent colleague Tamara Dickson brought to the book levelheadedness, an insistence on meeting deadlines, and a keen eye for sequence, nuance, and coherence. Managing three busy and headstrong academic types in a writing project requires maturity and toughness laced with respect and good humor. She has all these traits, plus aplomb, determination, and a cheerful spirit.

Frye Gaillard, noted Charlotte author and journalist, reviewed the manuscript in its entirety and suggested many improvements. Keith Pension, Queens graduate and trustee, missed her calling: she should have been an editor. I asked her to review several chapters, and the result was, in a word, superb.

Joe B. Hall, who played for Adolph Rupp and became his successor, critiqued the chapter on Rupp and gave us comfort that our treatment of Rupp was both accurate and interesting. Bill Lee's daughter, Lisa Lee Morgan, added immeasurably to the book by sharing many childhood experiences with her father. She also added insights into Lee's family background.

Les Smout, Jack Eckerd's financial advisor and executive with the Eckerd Family Foundation, reviewed the chapter on Eckerd and offered many valuable corrections of dates, names, and sequence of events. He shared the chapter with Ruth Eckerd, who found the treatment of her husband fair and accurate.

I want to thank Dr. Charlie Reed, William S. Lee Professor of History at Queens, who called my attention to Pindar's poem, "Winged Horses That Never Tire." This poem captures a major theme of the book and blends beautifully with servant leadership. Dr. Reed is a prolific writer on Greek histroy and was North Carolina Professor of the Year in 2000.

My associates at Queens's McColl Graduate School of Business, Barbara Wilson and Marcia Stefan, contributed effectively and substantially to reviewing the book and helping me juggle the writing project with other responsibilities.

At NewSouth Books, Randall Williams, Suzanne La Rosa, Mildred Wakefield, Rhonda Reynolds, Heather Finley, and Darlene Foster have unfailingly supported us in this, our second book with NewSouth. These are competent and nurturing professionals who are sensitive to the tedious process of taking an idea and transforming it into a completed manuscript.

Jane McColl Lockwood, Hugh McColl's only daughter, provided many interesting insights into her father and how he juggled the life of a famous banker with that of a committed family man.

Bill Grigg, Bill Lee's successor and confidante, added a host of stories on Lee, the servant leader.

To the trustees, faculty, students, and staff of Eckerd and Queens, a warm word of appreciation for the privilege of serving with you. And a special thanks to all of the board chairs with whom I have served in addition to Bill Lee and Hugh McColl: Philip Lee, Charles MacArthur, and Bob Sheen at Eckerd, and Joe Grier and Jimmie Harris at Queens—all servant leaders in their own right.

Finally, to the four principals—Hugh McColl, Bill Lee, Jack Eckerd, and Adolph Rupp—I owe a great debt and much appreciation for permitting me to join you in my journey over four-plus decades. It has been a wonderful learning experience to gain insights from you into the substance and craft of servant leadership. Fortunately, your legacies have become a vital part of the fabric of the endless debate about the essentials of effective servant leadership. We should all rejoice in this good news.